THE LIGHT OF THE WORLD
Essays on Orthodox Christianity

THE LIGHT OF THE WORLD

Essays on Orthodox Christianity

by

SERGE S. VERHOVSKOY

ST. VLADIMIR'S SEMINARY PRESS
CRESTWOOD, NEW YORK 10707
1982

Library of Congress Cataloging in Publication Data

Verhovskoy, Serge S., 1907-
  The light of the World.

  "The first three articles: 'Orthodoxy,' 'Christ,'
'Christianity' are translated from Russian."
  Includes bibliographical references.
  1. Orthodox Eastern Church—Addresses, essays,
lectures. 2. Theology, Eastern church—Addresses,
essays, lectures.   I. Title.
BX325.V47   1982   281.9   82-16963
ISBN 0-88141-004-7

THE LIGHT OF THE WORLD

© Copyright 1982

by

ST. VLADIMIR'S SEMINARY PRESS

ISBN 0-88141-004-7

PRINTED IN THE UNITED STATES OF AMERICA
BY
ATHENS PRINTING COMPANY
NEW YORK, NY

Contents

Preface

The main contents of this book are the articles "Christ" and "Christianity." The Apostle John says in his Gospel that were he to write down everything that the Lord Jesus Christ did, then "the world itself could not contain the books that should be written" (21:25). On the basis of the Holy Scriptures and the teaching of the Church, every Christian could write several books. My articles are comparatively short. They were originally written in Russian thirty years ago, in circumstances that did not allow me to give all the proper references, and their absence constitutes a considerable deficiency.*

My intention was to remain completely faithful to the New Testament and the teaching of the Church, although the brevity of the articles did not allow me to develop the ideas fully enough. The articles, such as they are, perhaps do not merit an English edition. My only hope is that some readers may possibly gain some new insight or deepen their interest in the themes touched upon in this book.

I am, of course, grateful to all the kind people of St. Vladimir's Seminary Press, who encouraged me to put this book together. In particular, I would like to thank my editor, Mr. Paul Kachur, for his patient assistance in the execution of the project; and Paul and Judy Garrett, who translated the articles "Christ" and "Christianity."

The article on "Orthodoxy" was originally prepared as an address delivered on the Sunday of Orthodoxy, March 7, 1971, at SS. Constantine and Helen Cathedral, Cleveland Heights, Ohio. "Catholicity and the Structures of the Church"

*In my book *God and Man,* published in Russian, much of the material is devoted to Christ, and I was able to quote the Scriptures as much as it seemed necessary.

was originally presented as an introductory paper at the Second International Conference of Orthodox Theology, held at St. Vladimir's Seminary, September 25-29, 1972, and was previously published in *St. Vladimir's Theological Quarterly* 17:1-2 (1973) 19-40. The article "Some Theological Reflections on Chalcedon" is reprinted from *St. Vladimir's Seminary Quarterly* 2:1 (1958) 2-12.

Orthodoxy

One hundred and twenty-three years ago, the Patriarch of Constantinople Anthimos VI wrote an encyclical letter to all Orthodox Christians, which was signed by all the patriarchs of the East and twenty-nine bishops. In this letter we find a passage that has deeply impressed both theologians and laity of our Church. It states:

> In our Church, neither patriarchs nor councils could ever introduce any novelty, because the protector of the faith among us is the very body of the Church, that is, our people themselves, who always desire to preserve their faith unchanged and in agreement with the faith of the fathers.

Thus, our patriarchs have recognized the great importance of the laity in preserving the Orthodoxy of our Church. We know that in the fifteenth and sixteenth centuries our laity indeed, under the guidance of the best hierarchs, saved the Church of Constantinople and South Russia from the Latin Unia, even though many of our hierarchs at the time betrayed the Church. In general, the great majority of heresies was started not by the laity, but by representatives of the hierarchy.

The same encyclical contains many ideas directly concerning Orthodoxy. For example, at the end of the letter we read:

> Brothers, our faith is not from man and not through man, but through the revelation of Jesus Christ, preached by the divine apostles, confirmed by the holy ecumenical councils, transmitted by the great and wise

teachers of the universe and sealed by the blood of the
holy martyrs. Let us keep the confession which we have
received in its purity from all these men; let us reject
any novelty as a suggestion of the devil. The Orthodox
faith is perfect.

Patriarch Anthimos insists that whatever is sound in the
faith of all heterodox they had originally received and kept
from the Orthodox Church, but by accepting also false teaching, the heterodox had, in his words, "dug by their own hands
a deep abyss between themselves and the Orthodox." The
patriarch does not hesitate to call the western teaching about
the Holy Trinity a blasphemy. He writes that "so many western leaders try and have always tried to allure us by words
of 'peace' and 'love,' which in fact are words of flattery and
deceit." But until the heterodox accept the true faith and
join our Church, he says, no real unity can exist between us
and them.

The late Archbishop Michael (d. 1958) of the Greek
Archdiocese has published in English another remarkable
encyclical of another Patriarch of Constantinople, Anthimos
VII, which was written at the very end of the last century
and which preaches the same ideas. "Without unity in the
faith, the desired union of the churches becomes impossible."
Anthimos also considers it absolutely impossible for contradictory doctrines to coexist within the same Church. And,
quoting St. Gregory of Nazianzen, one of the greatest fathers
of our Church, the patriarch states: "If our Church has to
defend the truth against errors, 'better is a praiseworthy war,
than a peace which separates us from God.' "

The patriarch also proclaims that "it is manifest that the
universal Church of God—which holds fast in its bosom
unique, unadulterated and in its entirety the salutary faith,
as a divine deposit, just as it was of old delivered and un-
folded by the God-bearing fathers, who were moved by the
Spirit, and formulated by them during the first nine centuries
—is one and the same forever, and not manifold and varying
with the passing of time, for Jesus Christ is the same yesterday,
today, and forever." And he quotes St. Vincent of Lérins, a

great Orthodox theologian of the West: "In the Orthodox Catholic Church we must especially take heed to hold that which has been believed everywhere, at all times, and by all."

When the holy patriarchs condemn novelties, however, they are certainly not defending a conservatism that excludes any development in the Church. Development is welcome; it is a sign of life. But it does not consist in the rejection of the eternal truth, which was once and for all revealed by God to the Church. As it was so well explained by St. Vincent, a truly Orthodox development must consist in an organic growth, which must be deeply rooted in the faith of the Church, in the Bible and in Holy Tradition.

Orthodoxy is nothing else but the total, sincerest faithfulness and dedication to the truth. The founder of the Church is our Lord Jesus Christ, who is the divine Logos (the Word), the personal revelation of God. He came into the world to reveal to us God, and the true nature and destiny of us men, and the perfect life which He has given to us. He called Himself the light of the world, the witness of the truth, and He said that He is "the way, the truth, and the life" (John 14:6). He came to give light to those who sit in darkness and in the shadow of death, to guide our steps onto the path of salvation. Where there is no truth, there is darkness and death.

If we recall century by century the history of our Church, we see that the first concern of the apostles, the fathers and the martyrs was to know the truth, to preserve it in absolute purity, to explain it in the right way and to establish the life of the Church and of all Christians on the foundation of this unique, divine truth. The martyrs preferred to die rather than to compromise. St. Maximus the Confessor, along with St. Martin, Pope of Rome, preferred tortures and death to the acceptance of error, which some of us probably consider of little importance. It would not be an exaggeration to say that our Church worships the truth, because the truth is God, and His only-begotten Son, Jesus Christ. "This is eternal life, that they might know Thee, the only true God, and Jesus Christ Whom Thou hast sent," says the Lord (John 17:3).

Thus, the knowledge of truth coincides with the spiritual life; ignorance, and, even more than that, false knowledge, is spiritual death. How can we be in communion with God, in Whom and from Whom is all our perfection, if we do not know Him, or if our knowledge of Him is wrong? How can we live in Christ if we do not know Him, or if we deform His image and teaching? How can we serve the Church if we do not know what the Church really is, or if we replace the true vision of the Church by our human imagination? How can we be moral if we have lost the true vision of man which God intended, or if we replace the true Christian ideal of life by the vicious immorality of modern disbelief or pseudo-Christianity?

In our Church, when we speak about knowledge, we do not speak about abstract theories. True knowledge is a participation in its object. To know God is to be in communion with Him; to know the Church is to live by the true reality of the Church; to know other men is to penetrate into their lives and to associate with them. Knowledge is absolutely necessary if we are to reasonably determine how we must live and what we can and must do. It is impossible to walk in darkness. True knowledge—knowledge acquired in the love of truth—is the first and greatest incentive and stimulation for living according to the truth. Christianity cannot inspire us if we have no knowledge of it. No one was ever saved walking in darkness. God, and Jesus Christ, is our Light.

I believe that true Orthodox Christians have a special grace from God, and this grace is love of Orthodoxy, that is, love of truth and love of the Church of truth. According to Patriarch Anthimos, Orthodox Christians are sealed by seven seals of the Holy Spirit, and they have been given a gift of obedience to truth. Thus, it is natural for an Orthodox Christian to accept the truth of Orthodoxy, being moved by faithfulness to God, Who is the truth and from Whom any truth is derived, or being moved by faithfulness to the Church, which, according to St. Paul, is "the house of the living God, the pillar and foundation of truth" (1 Timothy 3:15). It is not, however, sufficient to accept some truth only because it belongs to our family or national tradition.

There is a definite analogy between the attitude of a modern scientist and that of a Christian toward knowledge of truth. For the scientist, to know the truth means to know the reality of the material or organic world; for the Christian, to know the truth means to know what God and the spiritual world really are. In both instances, it is not a matter of someone's opinions or theories, but of reality itself. Nevertheless, the value of theology is often reduced to various doctrines, which are considered as having some authority or simply being interesting—as if the primary value of theology did not consist in giving Christians a vision and an explanation of the divine and spiritual existence itself! We need to know, and we can know, God, Jesus Christ, the Church and Christian ideals of life as they are objectively, in themselves, and not just human theories about them.

The teaching of Christ is the main source of our knowledge. Christ says that He knows God and His truth directly, and that he would be a liar if He denied it (John 8:55). St. Luke based his gospel on the information that he received from "eyewitnesses and ministers of the Word" (Luke 1:1-2). St. John the Theologian starts his famous First Epistle with the following statement: "That which was from the beginning, which we have heard, which we have seen with our eyes, which we have looked upon and touched with our hands, concerning the Word of life—the life was made manifest, and we saw it, and testify to it, and proclaim to you the eternal life which was with the Father and was made manifest to us . . . This is the message we have heard from Him and proclaim to you, that God is light" (1 John 1:1-3, 5). And St. Paul has the same consciousness: "I would have you know, brethren, that the gospel which was preached by me is not man's gospel. For I did not receive it from man, nor was I taught it, but it came through a revelation of Jesus Christ" (Galatians 1:11-12).

Thus, New Testament theology is not a human theory, but a description of the reality which was known in the direct experience and direct revelation by Jesus Christ or his apostles.

The Church has the same understanding of the authority of the fathers, the ecumenical councils and all the saints. For us, the fathers are not just prominent scholars, but above all living witnesses of truth, inspired by the Holy Spirit. To be inspired witnesses of truth is also the function of the ecumenical councils, which express the understanding of truth that is always present in the mind of the Church. And all the saints have had the same great privilege of having a real experience of communion with God, of having a vision of God and of the living truths of Christianity.

We often forget that the apostles ascribed to all Christians the possibility of a direct, experiential knowledge of truth. St. Paul writes to the Corinthians that "we speak the wisdom of God . . . [which] God hath revealed unto us by his Spirit: for the Spirit searcheth all things, yea, the deep things of God. . . . But he that is spiritual judgeth all things, yet he himself is judged of no man. For who hath known the mind of the Lord, that he may instruct Him? But we have the mind of Christ" (1 Corinthians 2:7-16). To have the mind of Christ means, evidently, to participate in the same perfect, immediate knowledge of truth that Christ certainly possessed in his divine and human mind.

St. John writes in his First Epistle that all Christians must believe in the divinity of the Son of God, and then he adds: "but the grace which ye have received of God abideth in you, and ye need not that any man teach you: but as the same grace teacheth you of all things, and is truth, and is no lie, and even as it hath taught you, ye shall abide in Him" (1 John 2:27). The grace of the Holy Spirit—life in God—is the highest and true source of our knowledge.

In his Epistle to the Romans, St. Paul ascribes the possibility of direct knowledge of God to all men. Whatever is knowable of God is indeed manifested to man; the invisible reality of God, His eternal power and divinity have been knowable for creatures since the creation of the world (Romans 1:19-20). Thus, if men do not know God, it is because they have become foolish and have "expelled God from their knowledge" (Romans 1:28).

The Son of God, Jesus Christ, has given us the real knowledge of truth. He Himself confirmed that the prophets were inspired by God, and the apostles, who were also divinely inspired, had no other pretension than to know, keep and transmit the truth which they received from Jesus Christ and the Holy Spirit. All other generations of Orthodox Christians, guided by the saints, the councils and the faithful hierarchy, have had in their turn no other goal than to keep in purity and true understanding the same divine truth, transmitted by Holy Tradition.

It is very important to know that all true Christians not only can learn the truth from the Bible and Holy Tradition, but, with the assistance of the grace of God, and transcending time, they can also spiritually become witnesses of all the great, eternal truths and great events on which Christianity is founded. In the services of the great feasts of the Church, we are always invited to come and see the events being celebrated, as if we would be true eyewitnesses of them. The gospel, read in the Church, has the same power and meaning as the preaching of Christ Himself. And in the holy eucharist we really participate in the Lord's supper and enter into communion with God and with the whole heavenly Church.

Many Christians in our time think that the only correct understanding of Christianity is a historical one. History, in their opinion, not only changes Christianity, but breaks it in parts, and in such a way that, in fact, each country and each generation has its own Christianity, which is incompatible with that of others. Consequently, they claim that it is absolutely necessary for our generation to also create a new form of Christianity. The continuity of a Christian tradition is said to be both impossible and undesirable.

The position of our Church, however, is completely different. We believe that there is one and the same Christianity throughout all the ages and that this Christianity is Orthodoxy. And the fact of a harmonious and organic continuity of Orthodox Tradition from the time of Jesus Christ and the apostles down to our own time is not only a matter of our faith, but it can be proven. It is impossible to find in the whole history of the Holy Tradition of our Church any crisis or spiritual revolution that would break the tradition or introduce any contradictory elements into it.

Two factors were necessary and sufficient for this achievement of Orthodoxy: the will of God to preserve in the world the truth which was revealed once and for all by Jesus Christ

and through the saints; and the good will of faithful Orthodox Christians in accepting and living by the Christianity of
God, Jesus Christ and the apostles, instead of creating a
Christianity of their own. It is not difficult to demonstrate
how all heterodox Christian denominations started by rejecting, at least partially, the true Christianity of the Church, and
later on how they passed through crises that deformed their
traditions more and more. It is, moreover, remarkable how
many denominations are identified with the persons of their
founders, e.g., Luther or Calvin, or how their theology is
shaped almost entirely by some individual theologians, e.g.,
St. Augustine or Thomas Aquinas. All this is decidedly not
the case with Orthodoxy. We identify our truth with God
Himself, and our faith with that of all the prophets, apostles,
saints and all faithful Orthodox Christians.

Orthodox theology gives us a whole and totally coherent
vision of truth. It is absolutely impossible to find any contradiction in it. On the other hand, it is quite easy to find
contradictions and confusion within the teachings of other
denominations. Only ignorance of theology—both the Orthodox and the heterodox—can bring anyone to the supposition
that what the theology of other churches teaches is as convincing and coherent as the teaching of Orthodoxy, or that
our doctrines and their doctrines are essentially the same. It
is enough to carefully study the non-Orthodox doctrines to
see the numerous false and contradictory ideas in them.
Perhaps there are some who would accuse us of what is now
called "triumphalism." But this is not "triumphalism"; it is
simply love of truth. And this love, which is the essence of
Orthodoxy, is a gift of God given to our Church. If Jesus
Christ our Lord said that He would be a liar if He denied
that He knows God, then we Orthodox would also be liars
and apostates if we denied that our Church really possesses
the truth. If we deny this fact, then we are no longer Orthodox. And if we believe in Orthodoxy without knowing what
is the truth which the Orthodox Church teaches, then we are
poor Orthodox believers.

If we are sincere in our love of truth, we must do our
best to know it as much as possible. To know the New Testa-

ment and the basic doctrines of the Church is an absolute must for all of us. For many centuries, one of the most effective sources of the knowledge of Orthodoxy for our fathers was our liturgical services. Whoever knew not only the Divine Liturgy but also the texts of the other sacraments, the great feasts, the first week of Great Lent and Holy Week knew at least all the essential teachings of the Church. Therefore, it is deplorable that in America there is a clear tendency to serve as few and as brief services as possible.

What are the greatest temptations undermining our faithfulness to Orthodoxy and clearly weakening our society? One is that, unfortunately, many Orthodox have hardly any faith and keep only external, earthly relations with the Church. Much more dangerous, however, is the wave of false theology with which the entire Christian world is being corrupted and which is inevitably penetrating more and more even into our Church. Some statements of our hierarchs and theologians no longer sound like statements of witnesses of Orthodoxy. The greatest danger is the almost open rejection of the primary and fundamental value and existential meaning of truth. Truth is considered as of no importance for life. Many think that a minimum of knowledge is sufficient for our activity, and that so-called "good relations" with our fellow men do not require communion in truth and faith, which is rather an obstacle for them. We are told openly that the entire teaching of the Church must be totally reconsidered and adjusted to one goal only, which is the immediate unification of all the Christian denominations in an absolute minimum of faith and in a common activity in this world. And this disdain of truth and the minimalization of faith is directly connected in our time with the conscious acceptance of immorality. Those who do not accept the moral principles of the New Testament will inevitably fall into immorality.

The secular activity in the world proposed for us by the so-called progressive Christians is, in fact, determined by ideals whose origin is manifestly non-Christian and which are preached everywhere by atheistic liberalism. We laymen must be active in the world, but let us act in a truly Christian way, with the Christian understanding of the problems of the life of our society. Let us not slavishly imitate those who are often enemies of Christianity.

Some Orthodox are so moved by sheer sentimentality that they are, so to speak, ready to kiss the heterodox and recognize their supposed "Orthodoxy," as if by such spectacular actions and superficial proclamations of unity all Christians, so deeply disunited for centuries, can suddenly become members of one Church! Furthermore, some Orthodox think that if they will establish the best possible relations with Western Christians, diluting the Orthodox faith in the sea of ecumenism, then they will be helped by these Western Christians in the extremely difficult situations in which many of our Orthodox churches now find themselves. This, however, is pure illusion. The West did not save us from the Moslems in the fifteenth century, and it will not save us from any of our present terrible troubles. Besides, the very idea of betraying our faith to buy favors from the West is an abomination!

Love without truth is a false passion! Nevertheless, love is now being constantly opposed to truth. In the name of love, any compromise with the most obvious enemies of Christianity is approved. Pluralistic ideological promiscuity is being recommended as the best path toward unity. In the opinion of many modern Christians, love justifies any sexual immorality, any cynical leniency toward crimes. But anything that is built on false compromises will not survive. Truth is not an abstraction—it is the source of life. According to the Scriptures, the tree of life is wisdom.

Freedom is one of the greatest gifts of God to the human being. But freedom is also as terribly abused by the modern mind as is love. The positive meaning of truth is to be free from evil and for all that is good. However, freedom is too often identified with arbitrariness and its negative use: freedom from God, freedom from truth, freedom from the love of the Church, freedom from any principles. We would do well to remember the words of St. Paul: "The Lord is the Spirit: and where the Spirit of the Lord is, there is liberty" (2 Corinthians 3:17); "Brethren, ye have been called unto liberty; only use not liberty for an occasion to sin" (Galatians 5:13); "All things are permissible for me, but I will not be brought under the power of any" (1 Corinthians 6:12).

Our love of Orthodoxy and our absolute dedication to it must not bring us to religious isolationism and by no means toward hatred of the non-Orthodox. We must be open to all Christians and to all men in the world; we must bring them the treasures of truth which we have kept for twenty centuries. Even when we cannot convert others, we can still enrich the non-Orthodox and the whole American society by our message. Whenever we meet other Christians, we must always appreciate them in the light of our truth. If we should discover in other Christians some elements of true Orthodox Christianity, we can enjoy with them a partial community in faith and we can act together, being inspired by that common faith. But let this unity be a true one, and not one imagined by ecumenical passion. The tragedy of modern heterodox Christianity is that, under the influence of modernistic ideas and trends, it often loses its Christian character. The unity that can be partially discovered with the great Christian denominations, inasmuch as they are still faithful to their own traditions, is no longer possible with the mass of modernistic Christians of all denominations. It would be no exaggeration to say that this modernistic Christianity is no Christianity at all. Real Christians could be united in a common opposition to the atheistic world and modern pseudo-Christianity.

There is no identity between Orthodoxy and heterodoxy. Whenever we see differences and contradictions between us and the heterodox, there is no other choice for us but to make a patient effort to clarify the errors of our heterodox brethren in a friendly manner and to try our best to bring them to the truth.

I would like to conclude with several references to the encyclical of Patriarch Anthimos from which I quoted in the beginning of this article:

Nobody will separate us from the love of Christ. Nobody will divert us from the doctrine of the gospels. Nobody will estrange us from the guidance of our fathers.

Wherever we will be—in the north, the south, the east or the west—let us direct our eyes toward the divine beauty of the Church.

Furthermore, Patriarch Anthimos says:

This apostolic exhortation and persuasion we send to the whole Orthodox society of the faithful, to the clergy and to the God-loving people, to the superiors and to the subordinates, to the rich and to the poor, to the parents and to the children, to the teachers and to the students, to the educated and to the ignorant: strengthen each other, withstand the devilish temptations, be vigilant and firm in the faith.

And finally:

The God of all grace, who has called us into His eternal glory by Christ Jesus: make us perfect, establish, strengthen, settle us (1 Peter 5:10) and grant that all those who are without and far away from the one, holy, catholic, and Orthodox Church may be enlightened with the light of His grace, and the knowledge of the truth. To Him be glory and dominion forever and ever. Amen.

Preserve, O Lord, the holy Orthodox faith and Orthodox Christians unto ages of ages.

Christd

I

Our knowledge of Christ comes from the living witnesses to His life—his apostles. The apostolic Church lived by their witness, which, in turn, has been preserved by all generations of Christians and confirmed innumerable times in the life of the Church. The principal expression of the apostolic tradition has always been the New Testament. If we accept the New Testament, we know Who Christ is and how He lived on earth. If we reject it, either we reject Him, or we confront the enigma of a man who lived as though He were God. The Christ of the New Testament and the tradition of the Church is both true God and true man; He is the Son of God Who became man. There has never been—nor is there now—any other Christ. Either Christ is God and the New Testament is true, or Christ was mistaken, entertaining a false belief in His divinity and in the Kingdom of God, which He ostensibly brought into the world for the salvation of man. In this case the New Testament is an absurd book. Some scholars and poets invent "their own Christs," selecting certain facts and ideas from the gospels. But who needs such inventions? Mankind needs the truth.

Everyone, nonbelievers included, should read the New Testament. But having read it, we confront the necessity of making a choice: to accept Christ or to reject Him. Upon this decision depends our entire life, or, to put it in a better way, upon it depends whether we will have true and eternal life or whether we will follow the path of perpetual death in error and evil.

The knowledge that believers have of Christ does not come

from the books of the New Testament alone—for He does
not live on the pages of a book. He is in each of us and in
the world, as our God, fellow man and Savior. We were
created in His image and, when we live in goodness, we live
in Him, even if we do not recognize this. Anyone who consciously follows Christ knows Him, for he lives by Him and
by His power and light.

The content of the New Testament and the tradition of
the Church is infinitely rich. In this article we wish to draw
attention to the most essential things found in the New Testament concerning Christ, hoping that the reader already knows
the New Testament or will desire to read it. We avoid references and quotations only because of space limitations.

II

Christ was born in a modest little house in Bethlehem, a
small town in Judea, to a poor working family which had,
however, once belonged to the royal lineage. At the same
time, the gospel tells us that this unknown child brought into
the world in a manger was "God with us."[1] He was born of
the Virgin, who had been overshadowed by the power of the
Spirit of God. Angels and signs had proclaimed His birth.

Christ grew up in the family of a carpenter and became a
carpenter Himself. He lived by His own labor with His
mother, among relatives, and "increased in wisdom and
stature, and in favor with God and man" (Luke 2:52). A few
people, though, already knew that He was no ordinary man:
at twelve years of age He had declared that the Temple belonged to His Father and had amazed the scholars with His
wisdom.

At about thirty years of age Christ went out to preach and
was baptized by John, who knew that the entire meaning of
his own life was in his role as Christ's Forerunner. During
Christ's baptism God Himself called Him His beloved Son.
Afterward, Christ fasted for forty days and was tempted by
Satan.

[1]Such is the meaning of "Emmanuel."

At the outset of His preaching Christ was completely unknown, but in time crowds of people began to follow Him,
for no one had ever preached as He did, nor had anyone ever
performed the miracles or the healings that He did. At the
end of three years His followers numbered about five hundred, drawn primarily from among the simple folk. Some
people were loved by Christ as true friends. Others aroused
his indignation and oppressed Him; at such times He would
seek solitude in prayer. During His itinerant years, Christ
lived upon the alms and aid of His followers, having no
shelter. He grew tired, He became hungry and thirsty, at times
He was sad and wept.

Christ preached the Kingdom of God, and that He Himself embodied that Kingdom, for He was the God-man—the
Son of God Who brought God down to earth, manifested the
truth and granted to mankind eternal life. At the end of His
earthly life the crowds of Jerusalem greeted Him triumphantly,
but a few days later He was executed as a blasphemer and a
rebel, reviled by the crowds and abandoned by almost everyone. The leaders of the Jewish nation hated Him. He could
have delivered Himself from His persecutors, but He had no
desire to do so—in order that by His death He might conquer
death and offer a sacrifice for the sins of all. Crucified, He
descended into hell as the Righteous One and conquered the
devil, who before had reigned by falsehood and delusion. He
led out of hell all those who were worthy of forgiveness, and
founded the Kingdom of Heaven. On the third day after His
death He arose. Even before His death Christ had appeared
to His disciples in His divine glory, but after His resurrection
He appeared to them in His transfigured body and talked
with them. He then ascended to His Father in order to send
down the Holy Spirit upon His disciples on the day of Pentecost and to found the Church. From that time forward,
millions of people have been saved in Christ's name, while
others have renounced Him or hated and persecuted Him.

The hymnography of the Church loves to emphasize the
contrast between Christ's human destiny and His divinity.
This contrast is a stumbling block for nonbelievers, but the
entire meaning of Christ's life and of Christianity as a whole

lies in the union of the divine and the human. For man is called to be a participant in the divine nature and life; we are called to live by the divine ideal. Only when we draw near to God can we be perfect. Only in God do we find unity with one another. And only God become man could save man from evil.

III

Christ was aware that He was the Son of God and the Son of Man. He accepted the title "Son of God" with approval. Only the demons were forbidden by Him to testify to His divinity. If Christ often preferred to conceal the fact that He was God, clearly He did so because too many people would either have been appalled by the idea of God's incarnation as a simple man, or have related to Him—as God—in a way utterly alien to what He wished. People cannot comprehend the concept of God's humility; the fact that God could adopt the simple form of our human existence seems an absurdity. People value above all else God's qualities of omnipotence, generosity and glory. They love to worship God not in spirit, in love and in truth, but through solemn and moving rituals with petitions for earthly blessings. Even those who were close to Christ expected an earthly kingdom from Him with places of honor for themselves in it. The people wanted to make Him king, in order to receive from Him earthly provisions and healing. Christ knew that the crowd that glorified Him one day in Jerusalem "in the name of the Lord" would five days later scream "Crucify Him! Crucify Him!" When man meets God, a tremendous amount of preparation is required. God's grandeur could stagger anyone, but being struck with fear at God's eternal power is not true communion with Him. God's true grandeur is spiritual, and we must ourselves attain a certain loftiness of spirit in order to accept God inwardly.

Each person is called to be a son of God. Christ Himself spoke of this and revealed to us within Himself the possibility of a perfect God-son relationship. In order to distinguish His sonship from that of mankind as a whole, Christ calls Himself the "only-begotten" (i.e., unique) Son, and never did He in essence identify Himself with the rest of mankind in relation to God. For instance, He says, "to *My* Father and *your* Father," not "to *our* Father." (Here, of course, we are not speaking of Christ's voluntary identification with us, which He accomplished for our salvation.)

Christ called Himself the Lord. We know this to be the principal name for God in the Scriptures, equivalent to the theophanic Name of Yahweh (which means "He Who is"). Thus, if Christ called Himself "Lord," this was equivalent to calling Himself "God," as His apostles openly did. Christ almost always called God His Father, but not in order to show that He Himself was not God. On the contrary, to be the Son means to have the same nature as the Father. To be born of God means to *be* God. While never fusing His person with that of the Father, Christ identifies Himself with Him by nature and in all the divine properties: He and the Father are one (i.e., one God) ; He abides "in the bosom of the Father." To know the Son, to confess Him, to honor Him, to see Him—or to renounce and hate Him—means to do so in relationship to the Father. Christ is the Mediator between God the Father and mankind precisely because in Him the Father is wholly manifested to the world. Christ is equal to God and like Him in all things: like the Father, He is unique (there is no second Father, Son and Holy Spirit), and at the same time He is "the Beginning and the End" (i.e., the fulness of being: "He Who Is"). Like the Father, He is free and omnipotent; He creates and provides for the world; He sends down the Spirit. Like the Father, He possesses perfect love, wisdom, holiness, eternity and omnipresence. More than once the Father bore witness to the divinity of His Son (for example, at the baptism and at the transfiguration), and Christ cited this witness. Being God, the Son possesses within Himself eternal life, which He can give to mankind. His being precedes His earthly birth. He existed before the creation of the world; He always was with the Father. Christ perceived His earthly life as a coming from heaven, from God, the fulfilment of His having been sent from the Father. He had to return to the Father when His work on earth was completed. Christ was aware that He was "from above" and not "of this world." He rejoiced over His return to the Father.

During His earthly life, Christ behaved as God. He performed miracles; He forgave sins; He transformed the decrees of the Old Testament. He maintained that people would be saved by Him and by serving Him, that all power was given to Him on heaven and on earth, and that He would come in glory to judge both the living and the dead, whom He would resurrect.

IV

The New Testament not only affirms Christ's divinity, but it also reveals to us His personal relations with God the Father and the Holy Spirit. Everything which the Son has, He has from the Father, including His very being. He is the image or Word of the Father, the radiance of His glory.[2] The Father loves the Son and glorifies Him; the Son loves the Father, and His whole life, work, thought and doctrine were all determined by the Father's will and thought. Christ recognized that the Father is even greater than Himself—not, of course, in the sense that the Father is God to a greater degree than the Son is, but precisely in that the Son's entire divine being is from the Father, and He follows the Father with His whole life, being His image and Word. The Father knows the Son and the Son knows the Father. This knowledge is a full spiritual possession each of the other; the Father abides in the Son and the Son in the Father. Why, then, did Christ say that the Father abandoned Him on the cross? Christ's abandonment is only relative. He was abandoned by God inasmuch as He died according to His humanity, for death is abandonment by the power of Life. But according to His own witness, Christ was not alone even in His sufferings. The Father continued to be with Him because, as God, Christ did not die, and, as man, He did not see corruption even in death.

[2]In the Greek New Testament, the term for "Word" is Λόγος—i.e., a thought formed and expressed in a word.

God the Father granted to the Son, from all eternity, His Spirit—the Spirit of His love and of holiness, of wisdom and of power, i.e., the Holy Spirit. The Holy Spirit abides in the Son from eternity and is even called *His* Spirit (although like the Son He proceeds only from the Father), for the Holy Spirit lives by the Son of God, having in Him the personal manifestation of truth and the Logos of God. The Holy Spirit is the Spirit of life, but without truth and wisdom there is no life. A life of goodness realizes and manifests the truth. Thus, the Holy Spirit, as the Spirit of life, is indivisible from the Son of God as the divine Wisdom. He is the Spirit of truth and of wisdom, Who manifests and realizes these by His life-giving power. Filled with the Spirit, Christ can grant and send Him from the Father. In turn, the Holy Spirit sends Christ into the world and witnesses to His divinity.

V

It is sufficient to recognize that Christ was truly God in order to comprehend the rationality of much of what people consider to be irrational in the gospel. Christ had to be born of the Virgin because it was fitting that the God-man be born of a human being by the power of the Spirit of God. Are miracles impossible for an almighty God? Only those who reject the existence of God can fail to believe in miracles. It was natural for God to declare His divinity in His baptism and transfiguration, which were manifestations of His glory and power. If God came to earth, it is understandable that the Kingdom of God was revealed for man, that eternal life, truth and holiness became accessible to him. God could not be conquered by evil; neither death nor the devil could conquer Christ. Being God, He had to rise and become the first-born of the saved and renewed human race.

VI

Not only was Christ true God; He was true man as well.

We have already indicated the facts concerning Christ as man revealed in the gospels. Can we doubt the authenticity of Christ's humanity and think, as did the ancient docetists, that it was merely imaginary? The New Testament clearly confessed that Christ is man, calling Him man, or the Son of Man. It confirms that He grew, that He was fed, that He slept, that He grew tired, that He suffered. If it is impossible to deny the reality of Christ's physical life, His spiritual and emotional life is no less obvious. We know that He experienced all that we do: He either desired something or did not desire it; He either approved of something or became indignant about it; He loved; He knew things, and there were even things He did not know, etc. Most importantly, the gospel informs us that Christ suffered *spiritually* (God cannot suffer in His own nature). In particular, Christ's expression "My soul is exceedingly sorrowful, even unto death" (Matthew 26:38) is inapplicable to God, for God has no soul, and in Him there can be nothing mortal, for He is pure life. The Son of God truly suffered, but precisely as a man, in our soul and in our flesh.

The Church teaches that as a man Christ is consubstantial with us. This means first of all that He has the exact same human nature as do all people. But it also means more. Christ is inwardly united with us. Of course, this union is made possible because Christ is joined by nature to everything human, but spiritual unity presupposes His free desire, love and knowledge. By the power of His love and knowledge Christ embraces all mankind in His soul. He possesses each of us in Himself and lives the life of us all. All of humanity is united in Christ and lives a new life in Him, just as He also lives in this humanity. Men are called to form a single being, like the Holy Trinity. But we can attain this ideal only because it has already been realized in Christ. And only because Christ indeed united all things in Himself could He transform, save and redeem all of us in Himself.

VII

Christ traversed the whole path of man: from earthly

birth to the transition through death to heavenly life in expectation of the universal transfiguration of the world. If Christ lived our human life in order to prepare the Kingdom for us, *we* must likewise follow in His footsteps. Christ illumined and consecrated man's entire earthly path. That is, He made it possible for our own life to be meaningful, good and full of grace, one which can lead us to God and to His eternal Kingdom.

Being God, Christ alone of all mankind was born of a virgin, but He Himself affirmed not only that God established marriage, but also that God Himself unites the man and the woman. Christ honored the marriage at Cana with His presence. Does not the symbolic meaning of the changing of water into wine lie in the endowment by Christ of sacramental grace on natural marriage? In any case, by His birth and infancy Christ consecrated maternity, birth and childhood. He loved children because He loved people, life, purity, humility and simplicity. The new birth is the new man, the new life. "Except ye be converted, and become as little children, ye shall not enter into the Kingdom of Heaven. Whosoever therefore shall humble himself as this little child, the same is greatest in the Kingdom of Heaven. And whoso shall receive one such little child in My name receiveth Me" (Matthew 18:3-5).

In general, Christ conceived of the relationship of man to God as that of children to their father. Sonship in the spiritual sense is receptivity, devotion, obedience, humility, purity, faith and confidence in the Father's love and care.

Up until the age of thirty Christ lived in a simple family, taking part in all of its labors. This fact has an enormous significance. Throughout history we find in people an ineradicable tendency to view common labor as just an unfortunate necessity which, though it may be inevitable, yet just as inevitably renders our life wretched, boring and humiliating. Christ's example shows that common labor is not humiliating and, most importantly, that it is compatible with even the most profound inner life. People usually think that a spiritual life is possible only in cultured people and in priests, monks, etc. Of course, the spiritual life does presuppose some degree of spiritual culture and concentration upon that which is above, but it is, of course, no less possible for working people than it is for the representatives of the upper class. Christ and the apostles found wealth and power to be dangerous for one's spiritual life. The educated Scribes were among Christ's prime enemies; His followers, for the most part, came from among the common people.

Family life seems to many people to be connected with fuss, banality and boredom; it therefore weakens and humiliates man. But over ninety percent of Christ's life was spent with His parents[3] among their close relatives. It appears that for Him this life provided the best environment in which to grow up and prepare Himself for the higher ministry that would require Him to abandon normal life.

Christ began the activity of His ministry by being baptized, by fasting and by repudiating the devil. It is difficult for us to say just how necessary Christ the man found this to be, but we do know that all of this was necessary for us. The Lord's baptism was a manifestation of the All-Holy Trinity, the anticipatory consecration—in Christ—of all of human nature and of the element of water. At the same time, Christ's baptism anticipated the establishment of our sacrament of baptism. Christ's fasting confirmed for us the real necessity of fasting, in order to test ourselves and to concentrate spiritually. Christ's three temptations show us the three main temptations that confront all man: material goods, vanity and the love of power. He rejects them not by the power of His omnipotence, nor does He simply drive the devil away—He opposes him with three sayings from the Scriptures upon which all people can lean: "Man doth not live by bread alone, but by every word that proceedeth out of the mouth of the Lord doth man live" (Deuteronomy 8:3);[4] "Ye shall not tempt the Lord your God" (i.e., do not use divine gifts for

[3]Joseph was Christ's father as far as the Law and societal relations were concerned. It is worth noting the fact that the Most Holy Virgin Mary lived with Christ for thirty years as a mother and "housewife."

[4]By the expression "word that proceedeth out of the mouth of the Lord," one may understand the Holy Scriptures, or, in general, all truth and wisdom, which God reveals to us. Man must be nourished by truth, as spiritual bread; he cannot live without it.

vanity's sake—Deuteronomy 6:16); and "Thou shalt fear the Lord thy God, and serve Him" (Deuteronomy 6:13). No worldly goods should force us to worship evil.

Christ's ministry was the preaching of truth. We cannot help but draw from this the conclusion that to preach the truth is the highest activity open to man in this world. The word of truth is the principal weapon in the battle for good. Simple discussion prompted Christ to speak about the truth. He did not shrink from sitting at the table of the sinner—for it gave Him an opportunity to teach people. At the same time as He preached, Christ healed people, comforted them, fed the hungry and drove out demons. Preaching was Christ's vocation. Doing good deeds was not His original goal—he simply did good deeds whenever the opportunity presented itself. Thus, a general law can be derived for all those who live in this world: pursue your own vocation, do good whenever possible.

People consider it to be immeasurably better to rule than to serve. But Christ came in order to serve, not to rule, and He said that it is more blessed to give than to receive. In serving we make others richer, we make them more perfect and happier and we turn them toward love. Thus, in giving ourselves and that which we possess to others, we gain those to whom we have done so. Thus, through His ministry Christ gained the Church, in which millions of people give themselves to Him.

Christ had disciples. He was the One sent from God in order to send others into the world. Being Himself the image of God, Christ wished to imprint His own image upon all people and to join them to Himself. The spirit of Christianity is one of ministry, of mission, of teaching and of active influence. To shut oneself up in one's shell means to betray Christ.

Christ accepted all of the natural ties by which people live upon earth. He did not reject domestic or familial relationships, nor friendship, nor His native land. But it is amazing how He elevated spiritual ties above natural ones. Christ's disciples are greater than His relatives; those who keep the word of God are more blessed than His mother. In large measure, His native people—the Jews—remain outside the

Kingdom, while a multitude of people "shall come from the east and west" (Matthew 8:11) and enter it, for they have perfect faith. There should be a correspondence between natural ties and spiritual ones (people who are related *ought* to be spiritually close), but even where there is no familial or national proximity, *spiritual* unity is nevertheless both possible and indispensable.

Christ did not reject the state, but neither did He exalt it. Securing political or social reforms was obviously not Christ's primary goal, but His words, "Render therefore unto Caesar the things which are Caesar's" (Matthew 22:21), can hardly mean no more than "it is permissible for one to pay taxes." These words may be taken more broadly—as a commandment to fulfil one's civic duty, and each Christian is undoubtedly called upon to fulfil these civic duties in a Christian spirit and with a Christian understanding of human relationships.

As a human being, Christ grew up in the Old Testamental Church, and He never rejected the Old Testament as a whole. He perceived in it the path to the Kingdom of God, which He would establish by His coming. The highest aspirations of the spirit of the Old Testament found their realization in Christ. In the same way, all that was limited in the Old Testament was bound to fall away. The Old Testament tolerated many things, condescending to the people's "hard-heartedness," but Christ made perfect truth[5] the measure of life in His Kingdom. The Old Testament focused most of its attention on man's behavior; Christ considered man's *inner* state to be the more important. The Old Testament is primarily linked with the Hebrew nation, whose purpose it was to make it possible for Christ to find upon earth at least five hundred disciples capable of becoming the leaven of the Church. But Christ wanted to bring into His Kingdom not only His own nation, but all of humanity. He accepted the dogmatic teaching of the Old Testament, but completed it with the sublime truth of the Holy Trinity and of His own incarnation. He accepted the hierarchy of the Old Testament,

[5]For example, Christ annuls divorce, which was tolerated by Moses' condescension. Christ rejected all human custom invented in order to soften the strictness of the Law.

which ought to have been the very first to enter the New Testamental Church, but He condemned its depravity and utterly rejected it when it rose up against Him. Christ participated in the liturgical and cultic life of His nation, but emphasized that rituals and customs are lawful only inasmuch as they are religiously expedient, i.e., inasmuch as they further one's spiritual and moral life. Christ gave new content to prayer and suggested that it ought to be as simple and as bold as the appeal of children to their father. He spent most of His time in preaching, in contact with the people and in work—which did not, of course, preclude continual inner communion with His Father.

Christ foreordained the Church's sacraments, which had not existed in the Old Testament. Christ gave the world much that had never before existed in it. First of all He gave Himself to it, and in Himself unity with God and man, a new human nature, leading man into the Kingdom of God and making possible the unity of God and man. He gave us the Spirit of God, the Spirit of love and truth. But Christ did not wish to destroy and reject everything He found in the world. All that was good in the world received His blessing, for it came from God, whereas all that had been wounded or limited by the entrance of evil into the world had to be healed and improved by Him as far as possible; for all that is good leads to the Kingdom of Christ. However, it is absolutely obvious from the New Testament that Christ's primary goal was to create an inner spiritual world in which human souls would be united with one another and with God in a single truth, holiness, love and beauty. Christ almost never spoke about the forms that Church life should adopt, but He did reveal to us the full depths of its spirit. He spoke of truth and knowledge, but He referred to the Holy Scriptures alone, with no mention of any other books or of science. He demonstrated the path of holiness, truth and love, but gave only the most general instructions concerning external behavior. Christ said nothing about art, but within the image of God and man which He projects lies the bases for all beauty. This does not mean that Christ was hostile to all the forms of our earthly life, rejecting them in the name of pure spirituality; but He knew that people are capable of creating for themselves external forms of life, and then have a boundless capacity for being carried away by them and then for boasting of them. In that case, the essence of the spiritual life remains scarcely even accessible. Christ saw true spiritual reality as life lived in common with God and men in love, truth and holiness—rather than in external piety, good behavior, politics, science, art, etc., although these may well be necessary on earth. All too often people live by all of this, thinking that they have thereby already become spiritual. Christ's prime goal was undoubtedly to demonstrate to us the genuine spiritual content of life, which makes all else seem secondary by comparison.

Christ was the Righteous One, and His righteousness was first of all inner holiness. Those who admired ostentatious formal piety were shocked by the fact that Christ was a simple carpenter Who had lived in Galilee, an area that had no reputation for precise pharisaic observance of the Law. They were scandalized by His breaking of the Sabbath, by His eating and drinking with sinners, by His not fasting as did the Pharisees, etc. At the same time, while Christ rarely took human conventions into consideration, even the most inconspicuous of His deeds was, in fact, always righteous. Christ's outward appearance itself reflected His holiness and purity, so much so that sinners repented when they saw Him, and anyone not obsessed with malice toward Him was involuntarily filled with respect for Him.

The final event in Christ's life before His death on the cross was His triumphal entry into Jerusalem. The significance of this event lies in the fact that good is capable of winning a temporary victory and of being glorified even in this evil world. Therefore, absolute pessimism, even within the limits of earthly history, is inappropriate. However, in this world, the victory and glory of good are short-lived. If Christ received no more than a single day's recognition from the crowds, how can the Christian demand more?

Christ died, crucified through the hatred of the Jews. Over the whole course of His life He endured the grief, the infirmities, the sufferings, the persecutions and the enmity with

which this fallen world is replete. While Christ endured evil
and adapted Himself to its consequences, He engaged in
battle with them. Not only did Christ's way of the cross have
the very deepest expiatory significance, and not only was it
a victory over universal evil, but it also sanctified and enlightened the way of the cross for all people. If we comprehend
the meaning of all that Christ endured, and understand His
relationship to evil, we will accept the fact that in this world
the cross is inescapable, that Christ shares its weight with us,
that even under difficult conditions a positive life is possible,
that with God's help the cross can surely bring us salvation,
and that if we suffer as Christ did we will become worthy of
His Kingdom. Thus, a person's entire life—both in its positive
forms and strengths and in its limitations and the tragedy of
the cross—is, thanks to Christ, permeated with an elevated
meaning and divine power.

If in Christ human life receives its true meaning and goal,
then to follow Christ's life and doctrine means to live intelli-
gently and in accordance with man's true purpose. Following
Christ is the first stage in Christianity. A higher stage is living
in Him, just as He lives in us. We must somehow identify
ourselves with Him, and hence with the ideal of life by which
He lived.

VIII

If Christ was both God and man, this does not mean that
in Him were combined two independent persons, the one
divine and the other human. It is impossible for two personal
beings to be united into one person. We know that several
persons can be united into one being, but not into one person.
Thus, the Father, the Son and Holy Spirit are one *Being,* but
not one person; a husband and wife and their children form
one family, but not one individual. Consequently, Christ is
not a combination of the Son of God and a particular person,
Jesus. There is but one person, or "I," in Christ, and this is
the eternal hypostasis[6] of the Son of God, Who Himself

[6]"Hypostasis" has the same meaning as "person."

became man and lived a human life in His human nature.
This one and the same Son of God is both God and man.
Therefore, the Scriptures say that the Son of God was born
of woman (Galatians 4:4), or that He purchased the Church
by His own blood (Acts 20:28).

As the God-man, Christ possessed the utmost fulness of
life. All good things were in Him from all eternity by virtue
of His divinity, yet He increased in all good things as a man,
as He grew according to His human nature. All that was
human in Christ was joined to the divine and was, as it were,
elevated to the level of the divine being.

Christ is the Son of God, both as God and as man. He
was born of the Father in eternity, and as man He was born
by the power of the Spirit of God from a mother who herself
descended through many generations from Adam, the son of
God (Luke 3:38). Christ's personal relationship with the
Father also embraces His human life. When the Lord said:
"Thou shalt love the Lord thy God with all thy heart, and
with all thy soul, and with all thy mind, and with all thy
strength" (Mark 12:30), He was obviously stating something
that He Himself experienced with His entire being. Who
could doubt that God the Father loved His Son, even in the
incarnation? Certainly the words "This is My beloved Son,
in Whom I am well pleased" (Matthew 3:17) also relate to
the man Jesus, for this man was the most perfect of God's
creations, more worthy of His love than the entire universe,
which He had so admired at its creation. How could God
not love the One Who loved Him even to the point of
sacrificing Himself on the cross? Therefore, it was not the
Son of God alone Who sat down at the right hand of the
Father in divine glory following the ascension, but the God-
man. If the Son of God always follows the Father in all
things, then Christ's entire earthly life was directed exclusively
toward fulfilling the Father's will, doing His works, teaching
His truth and glorifying Him in life and in death. Christ is
God's Messenger as man even more than as God. As the Logos
and Wisdom of God, the Son of God was always present and
active in the world, yet He became the Savior and Redeemer
only once He had become man. Christ knew the Father also

according to His humanity—otherwise, how could He have proclaimed the good news about Him?

The Son of God is the Wisdom of God, but the Apostle Paul also teaches that the Lord was "made unto us wisdom, and righteousness, and sanctification, and redemption" (1 Corinthians 1:30). Obviously, He was made so in His capacity as man. The Son of God is the Word—the Logos—of the Father, but "the Word was made flesh" (John 1:14), and, therefore, both Christ's human reason and His word contained and expressed in themselves the divine Word. The Son of God is the image of the Father, but in His human nature Christ also restored the perfect image of God as it ought to have been inherent in us from the beginning. Christ was the Lord not as God alone, but as man as well. In His human nature He was also the only-begotten Son, for there is no second God-man. He was not only "the Firstborn of all creation" (i.e., born before the creation of the world—Colossians 1:15), but also the "Firstborn among many brethren" (Romans 8:29) and "the Firstfruits of them that slept" (1 Corinthians 15:20), i.e., the first Christian, or the first Man, the First to be resurrected for eternal spiritual and physical life.

It is remarkable how the New Testament ascribes Christ's divine attributes to him calling him the Son of Man—saying that the Son of Man forgives sins, saves people and will appear in divine glory at the Second Coming. Both the Apostles John and Paul speak of the Heavenly Man or of the Lamb slain from the foundation of the world. This does not mean that Christ's human nature existed from all eternity. However, the Son of God foresaw in eternity His incarnation and therefore always had within Himself the plan of His human nature and life. In this sense it can be said that the Son of Man indeed came down from heaven, and that Christ the man was God in His person.

If the Son of God is eternally inseparable from the Spirit and is fulfilled by Him, so the Holy Spirit also fulfils Christ's human nature and always abides in Him. The very word "Christ" means "Anointed," for Christ is completely anointed (i.e., fulfilled) by the Holy Spirit. God had already prophesied in the Old Testament. Christ lives by the Holy Spirit. He was conceived in the Theotokos by the power of the Spirit; He was baptized by Him and led into the desert; by His power Christ performed miracles, drove out demons and preached. By the Holy Spirit Christ "offered Himself without spot to God" (Hebrews 9:14), by the Spirit He was justified and raised from the dead (1 Timothy 3:16; Romans 8:11). As a man, too, Christ grants the Spirit, and the Holy Spirit, as His Spirit —the Spirit of wisdom and truth—continues all of Christ's work upon the earth.

Beyond a doubt, Christ displayed His God-manhood in His relations with people. He was attracted to people with all His being, all His love and all His mind. He penetrated into each person's soul, and knew all that went on within it. He abides in all of us; He takes upon Himself the sins of all; He restores in Himself the image of each person. But we know from experience just how limited we are in uniting ourselves with other people—it is only with difficulty that the souls of others can open to us. It is with scarcely less difficulty that we widen the circle of people with whom we can truly live a common life. It is obvious, therefore, that Christ's love and knowledge could be universal only because they were penetrated by His divine power.

The body of Christ was of great significance in His life as the God-man. His miracles, transfiguration, resurrection and ascension were connected with His body, and in it were revealed His divine power, His authority over nature, His wisdom, His mercy and His glory. All of Christ's miracles had a spiritual significance, and in general it was through His body that Christ revealed His divinity. One must not forget that the word of preaching, which was so important in the life of Christ, was—as all human speech—a phenomenon at the same time both spiritual and physical. But Christ's entire outward life had a didactic and symbolic meaning—which is why the Church so attentively marks each of the events in His earthly life. Inasmuch as He became flesh, God became truly accessible to mankind. The ultimate medium of this accessibility is the sacrament of communion, which was established by Christ, through which we partake of Him Himself and of the eternal life that is hidden in Him. Christ's divine power overcame the natural limitations of His human powers, and overcame even death itself.

Through His body, Christ was in direct communion with the material world and laid the foundations for the spiritualization and sanctification of both our bodies and the elements of nature. It is the conviction of the Church that the very presence of Christ in the world of nature introduced into it a foundation of holiness and spirituality. Since Christ's coming, holy water, holy land, holy chrism and holy relics have all become possible, and, in general, it has become possible for matter to be withdrawn from the power of evil and to become a bearer of the Spirit.

The compatibility of God's sublime spirituality and the physical nature of creation was revealed with special force in Christ. It is not in vain that St. Paul says that "in Him dwelleth all the fulness of the Godhead bodily" (Colossians 2:9; cf John 1:1-2).

IX

How is the union of the divine and the human possible in Christ? It is possible owing to the fact that God and man are conformable. Man is similar to God—as a person possessing freedom, consciousness and a moral, cognitive and creative life; as a spirit capable of rising above time and space and of exerting dominion over nature. People are also like God in their capacity to form a single being without consequently ceasing to be a number of individual persons—just like the undivided Trinity. God's absolute perfection finds expression in man's limited perfections—provided human nature is preserved from evil and is submissive to God. In Christ we see simultaneously the purity of human nature and its total submission to the divinity. In Christ, all of God's highest properties are revealed in the forms of human nature and life. As the divine Logos, Christ has always been close to all creatures, especially to man—for He contained within Himself from all eternity the ideas of all that exists and of each person, and through these ideas or words, the Son of God has eternally abided and acted in the world and in all people. Hence, there is nothing unnatural about His having become man.

An analogy exists between the divine and human on the one hand and the spiritual and physical on the other. If the divine can be combined with the created, how much more readily can the spiritual be combined with the physical! Man is spirit incarnate; therefore, one of the goals of the divine incarnation was to establish a correct relationship between the soul and the body, to transfigure the body and to confirm that an eternal connection exists between the human soul and body. The whole of Christ's outward life expressed His inner life. His body was in perfect submission to His spirit, the obedient instrument of His activity in this world. Christ continually emphasized that the body must be subordinated to the soul, for the soul is immeasurably more important than the body. Thus, slavery to the body and its needs—affecting all of us who live on earth—seemed unnatural and unnecessary to Christ, even for His own body. God worries about us even more than we worry about ourselves, especially if we live by faith.

Poverty and persecutions forced Christ to experience physical sufferings and deprivations. Nevertheless, deliberate asceticism occupied a subordinate position in Christ's life—we know only of the forty-day fast that followed His baptism. In Christ's resurrected body we see the image of man's spiritualized body, which, though entirely real, had no need for food, nor was it subject to our laws of spatial limitations.

X

Christ granted us the possibility of eternal life. Life in the New Testamental understanding is not simply existence: one can exist and yet be corrupted spiritually and physically (i.e., die). Dying is the loss of one's strength and faculties; it is inner decomposition (equally of both the spirit and the body), a break with God, with other people and with the world. In general, dying is the derogation, disintegration and perversion of existence. What we call life is often, in fact, the process of dying. Living in evil means dying. True life is striving for perfection, for good, for the development of existence and, therefore, for oneness with God and with everything positive in the universe. We not only should exist eternally, but *live* eternally—that is, live in God, live in the Eternal One, also possessing in Him all things that are real, all good things. Life is love, knowledge, harmony, birth and creativity.

XI

Life does not exist in an abstract sense. What do exist are living beings, carrying out their lives creatively. The life of the spirit is fulfilled in freedom and responsibility. Freedom is the person's capacity for self-determination and independent initiative in his life. At the same time, freedom is also intrinsic independence from the will and actions of others. Where there is no freedom there is neither person nor spirit, rather just a thing or a machine.

It is obvious that Christ enjoyed freedom, and that in Him there was but one bearer of freedom, one free "I," and this "I" was His divine person. However, freedom could not be realized identically in His divine and human lives. Each of the divine persons determines His own life wholly by Himself; no one and nothing can constrain His freedom. On the contrary, human freedom is manifested by self-defense against constraints of all sorts—whether from our own natural limitations, from the world, from other people or from evil. Freedom is not license (that is, an action with no other justification than one's own personal desires). We confront a reality that has its own inherent law of existence, its own truth. Thus, freedom confronts the truth and has the choice of either following it or opposing it. Christ told the Jews, "And ye shall know the truth, and the truth shall make you free" (John 8:32). It is not within the capacity of freedom to be "free" from the truth; rather, truth—that light which reveals existence to us—grants freedom an opportunity for action and latitude. Freedom is meaningful and positive only when it is in truth. Falsehood seduces us, and leads to errors and destruction. Abiding in absolute truth, God possesses the fulness of freedom; but for man, knowledge of the truth does not come easily, nor is it easily followed, since reality is filled with falsehood and evil. But even as a man Christ knew the truth and was therefore free from errors and evil. Christ brought into the world a law which the Apostle James called "the perfect law of liberty" (James 1:25), because it is directed toward man's freedom, and wishes to confirm him in good without recourse to coercion. Christ accepted all the laws of the world—as long as they were not evil. However, He saw no necessity either in those laws that oppose the divine establishments, or in external directives that have no deeper justification. Christ recognized the religious and civil authorities of His day, but with one restriction: no power is higher than God and His truth. Undoubtedly, Christ did not feel Himself to be bound by anything earthly. He accepted only one thing, and that was the power of truth and love— but these He served with the full power of His freedom. He was free from the world in the sense that He was not subject to the anxieties and fears that fetter most people. Sins, sufferings and death horrified Him. Nevertheless, He went out to face them.

The Old Testament speaks prophetically of Christ as the Servant of Yahweh—that is, the "He Who Is" of Exodus 3:14 *et passim* (cf Philippians 2:7). What does such servitude mean? It means that Christ gave Himself freely to all—not to His Father and the Holy Spirit alone, but to all people as well, even to the point of accepting all man's sins, evil, depravity, sufferings and death. But Christ emphasized that His actions are free and that had He but wished to do so, He could have refused to continue along this path and could rather have destroyed His enemies, provided this had been compatible with the salvation of mankind. Christ's servitude is essentially servitude to love, truth and freedom, for thanks to it all of creation can attain the Kingdom of freedom, love and truth.

Many people cannot quite grasp just why Christ did not

use His omnipotence to establish His Kingdom. But for Him, only that which is free is authentic and valuable. That which results from the use of force is valueless and false. Christ forced no one to be good—because to do so would be impossible. No one can be saved against his own will. Christ laid down His own life in order to become the Way for all those who seek after true life. Those who do not seek after it voluntarily follow the path of death. It is possible to use freedom for evil; but freedom must serve as the basis for good as well, for without freedom there can be no good. Therefore, God, Christ and the Church have need only of those who are free; children, brothers, friends—not slaves—are needed.

XII

Truth is freely realized by a life of goodness. What is truth? Pilate asked this question of Christ, and it is sometimes said that Christ was unable to answer him. But Pilate simply did not wait for an answer; he probably thought that there is no truth—or that there are as many truths as there are points of view. Christ was the truth Himself, for He was the perfect manifestation of God and man. Many people suppose that truth is just our knowledge, some sort of human doctrine or ideology. But truth is reality itself, in its ideal form.

God is the truth, because He is the One Who Is, and He has a perfect knowledge of Himself. God is light, because in Him reality and manifestation are identical. He reveals Himself personally in His Son or Word. The Son of God is the living and personal truth of God in Whom is contained the divine idea of everything that exists. The knowledge of Christ is eternal life, not only because He is the Way to it, but because "to know" means to be in communion with. Therefore knowledge of Christ is entrance into the fulness of the divine being. Since the Son of God became man, we can penetrate into His divinity by getting to know Him as a man. Christ possessed a human mind and undoubtedly made use of all human modes of knowledge. It is natural for man to seek knowledge in God, whereas for Christ the whole of divine knowledge was open. Therefore, Christ's *human* mind was filled with divine truth. By penetrating into the content of Christ's thoughts, we comprehend the thoughts of God. No one can judge Christ's doctrine, for no one can surpass Him mentally. Being the Ideal Man, Christ contained within Himself perfect truth concerning man's nature, life, purpose and destiny. Thus, the knowledge of God and of man in Christ attains the maximum fulness accessible to us on earth. Of course, we cannot exhaust the fulness of Christ's wisdom.

Christ's doctrine supplements what we observe in His person, and His doctrine is not simply a string of thoughts concerning God, the world, etc., but a witness to the truth— a verbal image of the truth. Thus, Christ's words merge with His life; He lives in them as in His deeds. His word, and likewise His whole being, proceeds from the Father—it is "spirit and truth," and is filled with the power of grace. Following His departure from the world, Christ's word has been given to us by the Holy Spirit. In relation to the world, the eternal Word of God has a creative and ordering force, with an action that is immutable and unfailing, regardless of whatever changes may take place in the world. Therefore, Christ's word is the source of eternal life. In it is revealed and contained the truth, which sanctifies and transforms man by inward action upon his soul and life. This word is the seed of Christian thought and life. A profound perception of the words of God on our part is a condition of His coming to abide in us. God abides in His word, for He is truth; Christ's word is an emanation of His being, and through it He acts in us.

In preaching, Christ knew beforehand that few would truly become His disciples. But the action of the word of God is mysterious. It was not in vain that Christ likened it to a seed. One cannot say immediately which seed will germinate, or what growth of plant will develop from it. Christ preached even among hostile crowds, yet He also said that there is a degree of dullness and malice before which preaching becomes senseless and dangerous. Some people were capable of grasping only the parables, whose meaning was revealed gradually to them. Some believed in Christ immediately, being convinced not so much by His logic as by the power of His spirit, which was expressed in His speech, in His deeds and even in His outward appearance.

It is obvious that in Christ truth and wisdom are inseparable from justice or the law of life. Christ is justice or the law —although not a law of compulsion or formality, but of freedom and love. Justice is also holiness, and the essence of holiness lies in conformity with the divine law of justice. We also call "holy" those things which are dedicated to God and in which His power is mysteriously present. This latter sense of holiness can also relate to things (for example, icons, sacred vessels, holy water) that self-evidently cannot themselves be righteous. But for a spiritual being it does not suffice that it simply be dedicated to God and have gifts of grace— such dedication and divine gifts rather serve only to convict us if from them sincere righteousness (i.e., conformity to God) does not follow. God is holy because His life is perfect. As God, Christ is holy, while as man He is wholly dedicated to God and full of the Spirit. Thus, in His human life He has revealed to us a perfect example of righteousness by observing all of the Father's commandments.

XIII

The first question that confronts every free being is this: do you want to live by yourself alone, by your own personality, your own arbitrary rule, your own opinions; or, are you willing to find good not in yourself alone but also in others, and in reality, as it exists positively, in itself? The first path is one of pride and loneliness, of setting oneself in opposition to everything else; it is the path of contriving, quite arbitrarily, one's own truth and beauty, one's own good—which amounts to but ugliness and evil. The second path, however, is one of humility. People usually understand "humility" quite narrowly, not in its essence, but in its ascetical expression—in self-abasement, in considering oneself to be nothing, in emphasizing one's own sinfulness. However, the essence of humility as the basis of our whole moral life is realized when

we impartially evaluate ourselves and everything else in the
light of absolute truth, when we relate to everything that
exists—even the most insignificant thing—as good, and seek
communion with them not because we find them necessary
for our existence, or because we stand to profit by them or
gain pleasure from them, but because they are valuable in
and of themselves. My good lies in what is good for all;
my life is life in union with all others; what is true, good and
beautiful for me is also that which is true, good and beautiful
for everyone else as well. My values must be measured by
standards applicable to all. This is the essence of humility.

God is not proud; He does not affirm His own being in
solitude; He is not arbitrary. In giving birth to the Son and
procession to the Holy Spirit, God the Father does not exalt
Himself over Them simply because He is the Source of Their
existence. On the contrary, all three persons of the Holy
Trinity are equal in honor; Each lives in and for the Others
in the blessedness of the triune life. Christ was not ashamed
of being obedient to the Father, because His very life is from
the Father, and the Father's will is righteous. To live in the
Father is for Him the highest good. In humility Christ accepted baptism from the Holy Spirit, and by the Latter's
power He performed miracles and offered Himself as a
sacrifice.

As God, Christ's existence is wholly blissful; it cannot
be equated with that of His creatures, nor does it stand in
need of creation. In His perfect nature and life with the
Father and the Spirit, Christ is inaccessible to and incomprehensible for us. But in His inexpressible humility He created
the world—knowing all along that the world would revolt
against Him and that He would have to save it by paying the
price of infinite abasement and self-emptying.[7] Other than
humility and love, what could have led Christ to the incarnation and the cross? What great love must God have had in
order to endure death for the salvation of His fallen creatures, who bore malice against Him! Although men may

---

[7]"Emptying" or *kenosis* in theology refers to the voluntary obedience of
the Son of God to the human condition of existence, with its inherent limitations, sufferings and death.

doubt whether God is necessary for them, God, for His part, has no such doubt about desiring to grant us a life in union with Himself.

Being Himself the Wisdom of God, Christ perceives wisdom and beauty in nature, in the Scriptures, in man's everyday life.[8] He was ready even to be accused by an evil servant. He shunned nothing and no one—neither the faithfulness of the fishermen whom He had chosen, nor the children, nor Lazarus' humble family, nor the hospitality of publicans and Pharisees, nor even to be anointed with the sinful woman's tears. He appreciated everything good—be it no more than a cup of cold water or the widow's mite. The Son of God did not find it shameful to abide—as the Logos—even in the *fallen* creation, and to be its eternal Lamb and Redeemer.

Christ's external humble love for His creatures was realized in a special way in His earthly life. But there is no need for us to speak of this here—let each of us but recall the history of the gospel, from the annunciation to the ascension. The highest expression of Christ's humility is, of course, His death on the cross. Each manifestation of His humility can be explained by the way in which He condescended to all living beings, down to the last sinner, for the slightest good. But Christ's humility did not prevent Him from confirming His divinity or His superiority over all people. This is because when one is truly humble one does not depreciate oneself; rather, one simply refuses to depreciate *others*. Why, then, did Christ refuse to manifest His omnipotence on earth, to establish His lordship and glory? Obviously, because He wanted to manifest the truly divine heights of humility which mankind had so despised. Humility is the foundation of good —just as pride is the foundation of evil. Fulness of being belongs to the humble, for they are ready to love everything that exists, whereas those who are proud wish to live by themselves and thereby become empty.

Why do the humble avoid external conflict with those who are evil? Because they are prepared to perceive even in them a bit of good, which they are afraid of destroying

[8]The vast majority of the Lord's parables and the analogies that he made were taken from everyday human life.

together with the evil. True humility is revealed precisely by
the refusal on the part of God, Christ and His disciples to
think that evil people should be destroyed—or should never
even have been born. Only evil *per se* must be destroyed.
There is at least a single drop of good in each part of creation, and therefore God creates—and endures—even those
who deliberately become evil.

XIV

Humility naturally gives rise to love, for it is natural for
one to love those things in which one finds something good.
Love is striving to live a life of unity with other people, of
giving oneself to others, of possessing them. He alone truly
loves God, other people, the truth, good, beauty, etc., who not
only takes from others and uses them, but who in turn gives
of himself to others. It is true, however, that love is also
possession, for if I do not possess something, how then can
I be one with it? One may also legitimately love oneself, for
it is natural to wish to possess and live by oneself. Hatred of
oneself is the path of suicide. The hatred of oneself of which
the gospel speaks, however, is either hatred of one's sinfulness
or a readiness to sacrifice oneself out of love for someone
else. Misdirected self-love begins when love for oneself excludes love for others.

Love is the basic power of life. If one loves nothing and
no one—oneself included—why then live? Every act of life
is a relationship with something, but without love it becomes
lifeless. If love is truly a positive and comprehensive striving
toward the one whom we love, then it is at the same time the
most perfect act of life. We all know that the relations that
are permeated with love or the deeds done with love are the
most perfect.

The Son of God is filled with love for the Father and the
Holy Spirit. But He also loves His creation—He creates it,
He provides for it, He becomes its Savior. Because it was
united with divine love, Christ's human love on earth had the
infinity and the power of which man is incapable.

Christ loved His mother and His relatives, but for Him the spiritual family of those who are united in God superseded His earthly family. However, it is surely possible among Christians for the earthly family to be a spiritual family as well.

Christ had friends. Such markedly friendly relationships probably arose between Christ and those who were especially receptive to Him: the Apostle John, or Mary the sister of Lazarus, for example. In a certain way, Christ held John the Baptist in reverence; the bond between them was extremely profound and mysterious, as was later to be the one between Christ and the apostles—Peter, John and Paul in particular. During the course of Christ's earthly life, the apostles were primarily His *disciples.* However, between the Teacher and His pupils there was not even a hint of a purely "business-like" relationship. Their love and affection for one another touched all things—both divine and human, simple and profound. Christ entered, as it were, ever deeper and deeper into the souls of His disciples, until their lives became once and for all united with His life, in the same Spirit and love.

Christ loved His nation. Seeing its apostasy and foreseeing the calamities that would befall it, He grieved over it. To the women who wept for Him He said better they should weep for themselves and their children. He prayed even for His countrymen who crucified Him. Christ never let an opportunity pass, however, to emphasize that there are good people in all nations, that many foreigners are even better than the Jews, and that all people can become worthy of entering His Church.

Christ was surrounded by crowds. He knew the value of the crowd, but He saw within it individuals in need of spiritual and physical help and unable to find it. Christ taught the people, He fed them, He healed them, He resurrected them. He drove out demons from them, He comforted them, He struck fear into them, He convicted them of the evil they did, He rejoiced over them, and He saved them. He was moved with compassion and a desire to steer people—by word and deed—onto the path of true life. The love that stimulates good must be inwardly inspired by the highest ideal. Hence,

Christ spoke of good in the name of God, or in His own
name, or even in the name of a prophet. Love ought to have
a goal and content. Our union with one another is accomplished in something quite concrete, and the higher and more
solid this "something" is, the higher and more solid will our
bond itself be. Therefore, the most perfect unity possible between human beings is unity in Christ. In doing good, Christ
never demanded thankfulness from anyone—although He
considered this to be altogether natural and proper.

Every misfortune evoked compassion in Christ, which
made His attitude toward sinners very special. While never
justifying their sin, He had a special love for sinners, and
worried more about them than about those who were righteous.[9] It was precisely for the sake of sinners that Christ
came into the world. Love for our enemies can serve as a
measure of our love in general, for it requires such power of
humility and selflessness that it overpowers the evil that is
openly directed against us. Evil men were incapable of con-
quering Christ spiritually by awakening in Him a hatred for
themselves (i.e., by poisoning Him spiritually). Hatred must
be directed against evil *per se;* to hate the evil person is to
confuse good and evil, for even in those who are evil some
good is present.

Christ shared not only people's suffering, but their joys as
well. More than anything else, of course, He rejoiced at the
salvation of the world—even though this had to be accomplished at the price of His own sufferings and death. He also
rejoiced at each sinner who repented, at every good deed; He
shared the joy of parents who received their children healed
from disease or sin; He rejoiced with them at the birth of a
child, or at a marriage; He rejoiced when a shepherd found
his sheep, and even when a woman found her coin.

It would be incorrect to think that Christ's love was
directed only toward those people whom He met, or that He
paid attention to their external destiny alone. Christ's love

[9]The very term "righteous man" ("he who has no need of repentance")
sounds almost ironic in Christ's speech, because such a "righteous man" was
the self-satisfied Pharisee, whom it was as difficult to help as a sick person
who is convinced that he is healthy.

extended to all the people of the world who have ever and will ever live, and the goal of His love was to transfigure and reunite the whole of mankind and to bring it to God. Christ's suffering and rejoicing with others was primarily of a spiritual nature. Mankind's prime misfortune is evil, and its good fortune lies primarily in a rich spiritual life. Therefore, Christ's prime concern was to open to all the possibility of being delivered from sin and of finding the path that leads to the Kingdom of God.

Love is the means and essence of salvation. It is the means of salvation because only love can penetrate into the very depths of another person and see his ideal image—disregarding its present distortion and pollution. Only love can experience another person's life and devote its strength and its very life to him. The salvation of another person is a supreme labor which demands a supreme spiritual effort—not to speak of the external efforts necessary in order to help others. We usually concentrate mostly upon Christ's death for our sakes, but even before He died, His entire soul and life were devoted to us. Love is also that power which is capable of directing all that we have within ourselves toward serving our neighbors. The power of love consists in that, by spiritually possessing the one whom we love, we know this other person. Thus, Christ knew everything that takes place in people. Knowledge both illumines the path of love and is widened by it, until the boundaries of the two coincide.

Love is the essence of salvation, for spiritual unity is accomplished and brought to completion in love. Christ saved all, for He united all in His love. In His love for the Father and the Spirit He united all with Himself and all with God. The Kingdom of God is the kingdom of love, and Christ is its center. In Christ we participate in that love of God by which the Most Holy Trinity itself lives. This love of God contains both the essential knowledge of God and eternal life.

XV

Christ was perfect; and perfection is power. The word

"power" usually evokes in us images of external power. Without a doubt, if a person were to try to imagine how God would appear on earth, he would imagine the God-man as a King, Who by divine might would subject all beneath Himself and would establish by power a kingdom of ideal earthly happiness. But Christ took another path. Outwardly He displayed His power only in miracles, showing that His lordship over the world was possible. But evidently He did not want to make use of this possibility. His goal was to manifest the power of the Spirit in the Spirit itself, even under conditions of external weakness if necessary—and this weakness was to display with extraordinary clarity His inward power. Of what did Christ's spiritual power consist? It is the power of freedom, of truth, of beauty, of humility and of love; the power of peace and hope; the power of holiness.

Freedom is the condition of total inward power. The slave is powerful only inasmuch as he mechanically carries out the will of someone else. Creative effort ought to be free, and Christ's life was a great creative effort of the spirit for the sake of the salvation of the world. Christ's power was found also in His independence from the world. He feared none of the horrors of the world, nor was He dependent—as are all of us—upon its temptations, half-truths and lies. He did only those things which He felt to be proper in the light of the divine truth.

Truth is power, for in truth is found perfect knowledge. No error or deception is possible in truth. In the truth is manifested reality itself. Christ is the light in which each person can attain a perfect life; truth is life itself.

Beauty is power, for in beauty the perfection of existence is revealed. Christ attracts people perhaps no less by the beauty of His spiritual image, of His life and of His doctrine, than by truth or goodness. And His Kingdom is beautiful.

Humility is power, for anyone who is humble wastes none of his energy on avenging wrongs or satisfying his pride and vanity. The humble person is open to anything that is good, in whomever it may be found. Thus, Christ could unite everyone in Himself, despising no one, spurning no one, opening His Kingdom to all—even to repentant sinners.

The power of *love* is self-evident. In love all the powers of the spirit are united. Love gives a new existence, and, as the queen of life, unites all together. Christ's entire life was love perfected in truth. Love brought Him into the world; love united the Church around Him. Love and knowledge are eternal life, the manifestation of God on earth.

The power of *peace* lies in inner tranquility and unity, against which all the waves of the agitations of this life, undermining our strength and integrity, are broken.

The power of *holiness* lies in that it makes us inaccessible to evil, just as salt preserves from decomposition. Christ's holiness is a rock upon which a new world is built. Anyone who abides in Christ becomes holy.

Christ is the King, but He does not reign by outward power. He did not buy mankind by "bread"; He did not subdue it by miracles; He made no use of evil or coercion. He reigned in humility and love, by the power of the Spirit and truth. Only those who so wish are made subject to this power. All those in whom love and truth are found worship Christ sooner or later. In this is the pledge of Christ's victory: everything that is good belongs to Him.

XVI

The goal of the incarnation of the Son of God was not only to grant perfect being to people, but also to free them from evil. Only God become man could have accomplished this. Because a sinner *is* a sinner, he cannot free himself from evil. On the other hand, man is not a machine—in which case he could have been mended from without. Evil in man can be overcome only from within his freedom and nature.

The first condition for victory over evil is the existence of good. Sinlessness and immortality are inconceivable and meaningless apart from a positive life. It is impossible to fight evil if you are not grounded upon good. Indeed, why fight evil if at the same time you are not confirmed in good? In the morass of our fallen world, Christ alone is a stronghold upon Whom good can be built. It is also important that we note that in Christ and His Kingdom good is truly perfect good, with no admixture of evil. Without Christ people can grow in good, but only in Christ can good be realized perfectly. Christ is the new, sinless Adam, the founder of a new, holy humanity. However, Christ wished to unite us fallen people to His own perfect human nature. This could be done only by accepting our souls and by cleansing them completely in Himself, by renewing the ideal image not only of mankind in general, but of each sinner as well. Thus, in Christ, each of us finds himself cleansed and discovers the path to perfection.

Christ did even more than this. He identified Himself, as it were, perfectly with all sinners; He accepted upon Himself all the consequences of our sins and atoned for them. Sin carries with itself punishments, the main punishment being a rupture between God and creation. A normal relationship between the sinner and God is impossible, for sin is opposition both to God and to His law, the loss of conformity with God. God Himself cannot be with the sinner, for evil alienates God from him. Evil is abominable to God. What can God do in the heart of a person who is possessed with evil? To abandon God is to abandon life; man becomes spiritually exhausted and empty. Having taken upon Himself the sins of the world, Christ experienced our abandonment by God as His own, and He accepted upon Himself God's anger directed at us, as well as all of the insults and wounds—some of which are mortal—which we inflict upon each other. All of this was done in order to overcome in Himself our enmity and to reconcile us with one another and with God. Christ is the Reconciler, but He reconciles us by accepting enmity in Himself and by overcoming with His holiness and love our filthiness and hatred.

Christ's death on the cross is connected precisely with His atoning love. Guilt of any sort can be atoned for only by a perfect sacrificial love for the one who was offended. To do evil to someone means to manifest non-love toward him. We can repent for the evil we have done, but what will restore our unity with the one we have offended except love for him? It is not sufficient that one simply be forgiven; one must accept this forgiveness with one's whole soul and respond to it by striving toward reconciliation in the most profound way. Love is giving of oneself, the readiness to sacrifice. Therefore, in our world sacrificial love is precisely that perfect love which covers all sins, destroying them in us at the root. But truly giving oneself cannot be limited to the sacrifice of one's earthly life alone—it requires our entire being. Love should proceed from our entire being. But such complete sacrifice lies beyond the strength of fallen man: the more sinful a person is, the less capable he is of self-sacrifice. Therefore, only the Lord was capable of doing it: having identified Himself with us, He offered Himself wholly, in our place, as a sacrifice of love to God and to men.

If in Christ we manifested our perfect love (i.e., we gave to God our entire being), we deserve forgiveness and are reconciled with God and among ourselves. Christ's sacrifice is not only the sacrifice of an earthly life: in His love for the Father and the world, Christ surrendered to them His entire life and soul. His very death touched not only His body, but His soul as well. When He spoke in the Garden of Gethsemane of His sorrow "even unto death" (Matthew 26:38), He spoke, of course, not of the fear of death, but of horror at the evil that leads to our having to "lose our souls" in order to save them. If our souls are stricken with evil, we must renounce them, submit them to the judgment of God, mortify them and cleanse them from sin, and then receive them once again, renewed, from God. Christ had no sins, and neither had He any need to die in the flesh or crucify Himself inwardly. But He passed through the horror of the complete process of death, having within Himself all our evil, crucifying it in Himself and rewarding us in His being. Christ's death on the cross crowned the feat of atonement, but to the last moment of His earthly life, His soul and body remained inseparable in one single activity.

We have already spoken of the meaning of Christ's sufferings and death. Sufferings and death are unavoidable for fallen man. Proceeding from evil, they serve to limit it. But the real tragedy of human torments and death lies in hopelessness. Christ, being sinless, should neither have suffered nor have died. He accepted our path of death in order to unite it with the renewing and vivifying of our being. Not only did He destroy evil—He replaced evil by good. The light of His truth uncovers the most profound and subtle evil lying within us. By experiencing our whole life, He accompanies us on the path whereby everything in us that has been stricken with evil is crucified. By our sins we crucify Him, yet at the same time He by his own goodness gives us the strength that we need. Therefore, anyone who dies to evil is simultaneously resurrected for true life. Anyone who renounces pride or malice not only loses his evil passions, but also grows in the spirit of Christ's humility and love. Anyone who renounces false knowledge grows in truth, etc.

The death and resurrection of the body are like the death and resurrection of the soul. When the body dies, all that is diseased and corrupt in it also dies, and it is a perfect, spiritualized organism that will be raised up. Christ did not die of disease; He was murdered by evil. He accepted a physical death not only to fulfil His atoning sacrifice, but also in order to separate us from our mortality and to confirm and manifest in Himself the power of life over death. Murder is the last weapon and refuge of evil, but Christ deprived it of this power, implanting in our mortal bodies the seed of the resurrection. We must not forget, however, that the resurrected body will once again encounter suffering and evil if our soul too is not resurrected. All people will be resurrected, but not all will enter into eternal life—those who are obsessed with evil will go away into the world of eternal death, or hell.

The wide range of ways in which Christ related to sinners, not so much with respect to the quantity of their sin as to the nature of the sin and the humility of the sinner, is truly amazing. Christ forgave everyone in whom He saw repentance. The humble sinner—if only he knows the truth—is near to repentance, for his sins torment him. Not to forgive a repenting sinner would mean to confirm him in evil. Christ's condescension also extended to pagans: although their knowledge of the truth is but poor, they are able to follow the simplest morality.

Christ was also conscious of Himself as being a Jew, as

was His mother, John the Baptist and His first disciples. (Christ's genealogy in the Gospel of Matthew lists only two non-Jews: Rachab and Ruth.) He acknowledged the Old Testament and venerated the patriarchs, prophets and especially Moses. Christ taught that the prophets had spoke of Him long before, that Abraham rejoiced to see His coming, and that if the Jews truly believed Moses, then they would believe in Him (see Luke 24:25-27; John 8:56 and 5:46).

The salvation of Israel and the service of His own people were considered by Christ to be His first goal. Neither in His preaching nor in His deeds can we possibly find anything that could serve to undermine the earthly well-being of Israel. The people were often found listening to Him, rejoicing and flocking after Him in crowds. However, from the very beginning of His ministry Christ exposed and condemned the Scribes and Pharisees, who very early on conceived a hatred for Him and time and again attempted to seize Him and have Him put to death.

While acknowledging the Old Testament, Christ clearly saw its insufficiency, particularly in its moral teaching of giving in to the "hardness of hearts" of the Jews (Matthew 19:8). He accused the Pharisees not for their adherence to the Law, but because they added many precepts to it, following the "traditions of their fathers"—i.e., rules of their own making. Phariseeism inherently contains hypocrisy and disregard for moral purity, justice, love and concern for one's neighbors —for the outward replaces the inner. According to the words of Christ, the preaching of the Pharisees produces only a "child of hell" (Matthew 23:15). The Scribes Christ condemned for their legalistic theology, which unnecessarily complicates everything and which not only does nothing to foster growth in righteousness, but rather serves to "shut up the Kingdom of Heaven against men" (Matthew 23:13).

In the Gospel of John, Christ harshly criticizes and condemns the Jews who were hostile to Him, whom the evangelist calls simply "the Jews." Christ said that these "Jews" do not understand the Scriptures, and this is why, when faced with Christ's teaching, they do not accept it. They do not believe in Christ, they hate Him, and they reject His divinity.

In a sense they thus do not really believe in God and have
no love for Him either. Christ even told the Jews that their
Father was not God, but the devil—to which the Jews
responded by charging that Christ Himself was possessed by
a demon (John 8:44, 48, 52).

Christ placed the Kingdom of God above nationality, and
allowed the possibility that the pagans could turn to true
faith whereas the Hebrews, in spite of the great advantage of
belonging to the Old Testament church, could be "cast out"
of the Kingdom while the other nations will enter into it
(Matthew 8:11-12). The Jewish leaders therefore decided to
eliminate Christ, on the grounds that He was dangerous for
the Jewish state and people, whom He was corrupting by His
teaching (Luke 23:2; John 11:47-53). When Christ confessed
His divinity, the Sanhedrin sentenced Him to death, and
Pilate, in a cowardly manner, yielded to them and had Jesus
crucified.

Before His death, Christ had said that many times He had
wanted to unite His people around Himself, but they would
not have it so, and thus the Lord concluded: "Behold, your
house is left unto you desolate" (Matthew 23:38).

The Lord Himself said that He had come to the earth
in order to be crucified (Luke 24:7; John 12:27); He could
have avoided death and shattered His enemies (Matthew
26:53), but His death was necessary for the salvation of mankind. The voluntary consent of Christ to die on the cross did
not, however, take away responsibility from those who desired
His crucifixion. All men, of course, crucify Christ by their
sins, but much greater responsibility falls on those who consciously persecuted Christ and wanted to see Him die. The
Lord Himself allowed that those who crucified Him could
"know not what they do" (Luke 23:34), but it is impossible
to allow that all who took part in His crucifixion were un-
aware of what they were doing. "Woe unto the world because
of offenses! for it must needs be that offenses come; but woe
to that man by whom the offense cometh" (Matthew 18:7),

Death is necessary for men, for only by death can men
free themselves from this fallen, corrupted world and thus
begin a new and perfect life. In this connection, there is no

clearer proof of the complete corruption of this world than the fact that no place could be found in it for God Himself— even the chosen people not only did not receive the Son of God, but put to death the One Who had come to save the world.

XVII

For forty days following His resurrection Christ appeared to His disciples and spoke with them, completing their preparation for the ministry in the Church that lay before them. It was precisely at this time that He imparted to them the special gifts of the Spirit. Shortly thereafter He ascended into heaven. Christ's ascension shows that the full triumph of God's truth cannot yet come in this world. Until the end of history, this triumph is only possible in heaven; on earth it is possible only partially and invisibly. In Christ mankind is saved, truth and good are confirmed, and mankind's future history has positive meaning inasmuch as people commune with Christ and enter into His Kingdom.

The Church first appears after Christ's ascension. The Holy Spirit and Christ's disciples take a visible part in its foundation. By His power the Holy Spirit inwardly transfigures people, joining them to Christ and giving them the power of true life. The entire earthly task of the building of the Church belongs to people (although in conformity with Christ's doctrine and by the inspiration of the Spirit). Just how does Christ abide in His Church? He is her Head, and also her first Member. He directs the Church, having a mystical influence on her life by His divine power. He determines the life of the Church by His truth and His entire being, for to be in the Church means to live in Christ. Everything that fails to correspond to Christ's spirit lies outside the Church. Finally, we can communicate with Christ in the eucharist.

The New Testament describes Christ after the ascension both in His divinity and in His humanity—as the Lord, Who possesses the fulness of power and glory. However, Christ's heavenly power itself stems not only from His divinity, but also from the fact that He was the Lamb, Who had come to sacrifice Himself for the sake of humanity. He remains the Lamb forever, but He also became the Lion: the Conqueror of His enemies (Revelation 5:5). Christ's self-denial itself now gives Him an invincible power over all creatures.

In heaven Christ is surrounded by the faithful, who eternally glorify Him, yet He does not forget the world—He chastises the evil contained therein, and He does everything possible to save all Christians. Nevertheless, the final victory over evil is attained only with Christ's Second Coming with the saints. This final victory will be manifest and glorious, and also terrible for all the enemies of Christ, who persecuted Him even unto death. Judgment over humanity has been handed over by God the Father to the Son of God. Those who accept Christ and who have the good in themselves will be justified; but those who reject Christ and who are indifferent to the good will be condemned.

When the world is made new, the Lord will be entirely united with those who believe in Him—united as the Bridegroom with His bride, sharing a single, common life. He will be the Light of the world and the Temple, containing in Himself all of the saved. This new world is described in the book of Revelation as a world of bliss, and for this reason the ancient Christians awaited with great expectation, almost impatience, the Second Coming of the Lord.

XVIII

The Christian has but one God—the Father, the Son and the Holy Spirit. He has but one Lord—Christ. Christ is our Lord not only because He is a divine, perfect person, but also because in Him we see revealed the new world of existence and the perfect ideal of life; its true meaning is revealed. In Christ we have understood God, and God has become our Father and the Principle of our life. In Christ we have understood who man is. We have learned to value the richness of the spirit and its indivisibility from the body. We now know what life is, and have a basis for loving it—for we can hope for immortality, salvation and the transfiguration of everything good. In Christ we are already ascended into heaven and our soul is resurrected from evil. We ascend toward God through Christ, but God also sees and loves us in Christ.

Christ left us in the same world of good and evil in which He Himself once lived, and we ought to follow Him. We should have His Kingdom in our soul, and by His power continually draw nearer to Him even on this earth, carrying our cross and striving to make it the cross of Christ.

Christianity

I

Christianity is the religion that Christ preached and established on earth. It is the truth about God and the world, about man and human life as it is, as it ought to be and as it will be. Even theology as a whole cannot exhaust the content of Christianity, and this article can but say a few words about the most essential elements in it. The primary source of Christian doctrine is the Holy Scriptures, and the New Testament in particular. Nothing can replace a knowledge of them if one wants to know Christianity and live the Christian life.

THE KINGDOM OF GOD

II

The essence of Christianity lies in the union of man with God, of man with man and with the whole of creation. Christianity is founded in this dual unity, in which neither aspect of unity is divisible from the other. We cannot be with God if through enmity we are divided among ourselves, nor can we be truly united among ourselves except in God. Christ is the One Who within Himself united all with God. The vertical line of Christ's cross symbolizes unity with God, while the horizontal line symbolizes unity of men. The two lines intersect in a single point—which is Christ.

How is unity with God possible, and why is it necessary?

The human spirit is like God in all things, except it is not perfect. We can ascend to God as to the all-perfect Spirit, and He can descend to us as to creatures who are similar to Himself. He is the foundation and the fulness, the ideal and the measure of our being.

Experience reveals to us first of all our soul, that is, the world of our experiences—our thoughts, desires and feelings. Even the external world is revealed to us only in our sensations, thoughts and concepts. The whole of human life is primarily the life of the soul, although it is interrelated with the body. Without a will, intelligence and emotions, how could we relate to other people? How could society, culture and even the most rudimentary work exist? We concentrate most of our energy upon our external life, but the very fact that it is possible for the spirit to rule the body and nature demonstrates its superiority over them. In love, knowledge and creativity we can transcend everyday life. Knowledge of nature and contemplation of its beauty create within us an ideal image of the world. Our relations with other people— in that they have an inward, moral character—reveal to us the depths of the human spirit. In science and art we express all the riches of the knowledge and beauty by which man is capable of living.

If man were to confine himself to the spiritual riches that he finds in himself and in the world, he would never give God a thought; but in the spiritual realm man can never find satisfaction in his own attainments, and, at any rate, he realizes that no matter what summit of perfection he might attain, it can always be excelled. Who among us, without falling into blind self-adulation, would ever say, "My love is sufficient, my holiness is sufficient. I know enough. Everything is perfectly clear to me. I'm perfect!" On the contrary, we know that the more perfect a person becomes, the more he realizes just how imperfect he is. It is in this realization of our own limitedness, a realization which comes to us on the endless path toward perfection, that God is revealed to us. He is the all-perfect Being toward Whom we are striving; in Him is realized all that which we are but trying to achieve. In the light of His absolute perfection we see our own nothingness and at the same time the possibility of infinite movement toward the all-perfect.

It is important to understand that if man strives for perfection at all, it is only because he admits in fact that perfection exists, regardless of whatever theoretical convictions he might hold. Neither in ourselves nor in the world, however, is there perfection. Perfection can exist only above the world, in the perfect Being Whom we call God. Without God the human spirit is an absurdity, for all human moral, cognitive and esthetic life is based on striving toward perfection. If simply any level whatsoever of morality, knowledge and beauty would suffice, then no one would strive to attain goodness, truth and beauty; rather, all would simply lead animal-like lives, not even suspecting that there is something higher. The human spirit strives naturally toward perfection, as to its ideal limits. Therefore, all people find it simple to understand what God is, and it is always prejudiced, far-fetched and deceitful to deny the existence of God.

If God is a Being Who is all-perfect or all-good, then all perfections and all goodness lead to God. If there is no God, then neither is there any goodness or evil, truth or falsehood, beauty or ugliness; nothing at all matters, for there is no absolute measure. But if God does exist, then all good comes from Him and leads to Him.

III

The primary good is existence itself, for if someone does not exist, how can he make use of good things of any sort? And, whereas we all simply *somehow* exist, God is "the One Who Is,"[1] that is, He is the One Who enjoys utter fulness of existence, the One Who is Being itself. God's being has within itself its own cause or foundation. It is absolutely whole, indivisible and unchangeable; it possesses everything simultaneously in a single perfect, all-encompassing unity. All

[1]In Russian, *sushchit,* a translation of the Greek ό ῶν and the Hebrew *Yahweh.*

of God's attributes interpenetrate one another. Thus, for example, one cannot say that in God love is not wise, nor that wisdom is not permeated with love; nor can one say that His freedom is powerless, or His power without freedom, etc. God's life is not a death-like rest but a complex and yet unified, all-powerful act of being whereby He realizes everything that we, even through thousands of our own efforts, cannot attain. Thus, God is above time and space; He is eternal and simple.

Our existence, on the other hand, is not based within ourselves. In our existence, everything appears and disappears again; everything changes, passes from one thing into another; everything is divided, confused, limited, impoverished. One attribute pushes out another. The strong can be stupid, the intelligent weak; the good, ugly; the beautiful, immoral. Time and space more or less rule over all.

What relationship, then, can there be between God's existence and our own? We all know that our existence fluctuates between two contradictory aspirations: one leads toward the acquisition of a greater fulness of existence, and the other toward destruction and nonbeing; the one leads to God, to the One Who Is, while the other leads to the abyss of nothingness. There is a dark abyss of nonbeing in the world; wherever there is division—between two parts, between two moments—there is emptiness as well. It is the rule of the fallen world that there was a time when everything that now exists did not exist, and there will be a time when all once again will cease to exist. Yet, at the same time, even the tiniest particle of matter contains within itself tremendous power. The powers of attraction and repulsion struggle in the world in an unstable equilibrium. True equilibrium between them would mean that everything would be caught in a death-like immobility, while if one were to prevail over the other, everything would either disintegrate or amalgamate into a single point.

In the midst of all the contradictions in the existence of this world we are aware of the presence of a lifegiving and restraining Power, which penetrates all things in order to strengthen them and which diffuses everywhere in order to unite everything. When we look around ourselves we see things, plants, animals and people; and at the same time we see that everything consists of certain particles of existence swimming about in emptiness. Everything is at the point of disappearing, and yet, still exists and can even grow in existence, for the infinite Source of existence nourishes it in eternal renewal. God's presence in the world is evident to anyone who is not engrossed in the externals of the world and the abstract generalizations of science. There is in the world, and in everything that exists, something greater than itself. The world is powerful, wise, magnificent, and yet, in it is revealed another, greater Power, Wisdom and Magnificence.

God is not the Creator in the past alone; even now He is the Creator and Sustainer, and we are ever aware of His creative power. We confess Him, however, to be the primordial Creator of all, because He alone could create the world. To say that everything proceeded from something that existed before, which in turn proceeded from something that existed still earlier, etc., is to say nothing. If someone were to explain the fact of a hanging lamp by pointing to the existence of a chain having many links from which the lamp is suspended, and yet should maintain that the hook which in turn supports the chain is itself utterly unnecessary—such a person speaks foolishness. Atheistic explanations of the origin of the world are no more intelligent than that. Only God is the first cause, because He has no need of a cause in turn.

God *is* life; we *have* life. But life comes to us by continual effort; it continually vanishes into the past, collapses into a kind of darkness; and sometimes we even lose self-consciousness. It is as though there were beneath us a dark stream which we are attempting to cross by stepping from rock to rock, with constant effort and fear. On the other hand, not only can we merely exist, we can enrich our lives; we can become vitally richer and stronger and become greater than we are. The person who takes the path of perfection continually transcends himself—at times we can ascend in a few minutes to heights that can scarcely even be imagined. This is possible because in the very depths of our being there is an inexhaustible well of life, and from above there descends to us the One Who is fulness of being. Without God all of our desires, our reason, our heart, would dry up—that is, they would become petty, banal and evil. But in God we attain the One Whom we desire, the truth, goodness and beauty. Our life—inasmuch as it *is* truly life and not simply vegetation and movement of our body and spirit toward death— is nourished by its divine roots and is crowned by God. God is life; true life is from God and in God. This is one of the most profound, lifegiving, joyful experiences of which man is capable.

God is not only a creative power, the source of life. He is Himself *within Himself* the "One Who Is"—He *is* Life. He has His own inner life, which remains for us a secret, and which is not only perfect and good, but is beyond all the perfection that our thoughts and imaginations are capable of understanding. However, it is precisely this unapproachable perfection of God that attracts man to Him; only in God does man find a true goal and limit for his own life. However, God's superiority over man is so great that when we approach Him we feel as though we are being torn away from the world, as though we are leaving ourselves and are being absorbed, like a drop in an ocean of ineffable light, in the depths of divine perfection. But we do not disappear in God. In Him there is room for everything, and in Him we in fact find ourselves.

IV

Being means wholeness. If something becomes totally divided, it ceases to exist. Oneness is the foundation of holiness, as the realization of love. It is also the foundation of knowledge, because partial knowledge is imperfect. It is also the foundation of beauty, which is harmony.

In the material world there is no true unity. Matter seeks to be united in enormous clusters, stars and constellations, but at the same time all constellations, stars and all other

things are in a continual process of disintegration until ultimately they disappear. Why does the entire world not disintegrate? Every particle can be divided into parts, and there is
no end to these subdivisions. On the other hand, everything
in the world is united into greater and greater wholes, which
in turn are but parts of something still greater. A single universal whole is unattainable, yet everything that we see is
nevertheless relatively one. Someone's power is uniting everything—from the thousands of constellations to the microscopic
systems of electrons—and everywhere throughout the magnificent, multicolored curtain of this world we see the mysterious,
all-encompassing and lifegiving One for Whom there is no
difference between the atom and the universe.

Our spirit is united in our person, yet we know just how
difficult it is for us to control all the things that fill our soul.
What a multitude of often contradictory experiences divides
and weakens us! Our experience of the spiritual life teaches
that when man delves deeply into himself, seeking as much
inner cohesiveness as is possible, he finds within himself
something far deeper than himself: the fundamental principle,
as it were, of his very existence, which is the beginning of
unity both for himself and for everything that exists—that
is, he finds God within himself. It is easier to experience God
in the universe, but the more direct path to Him is through
the heart.[2] The difficulty of this path lies in the fact that we
attain inner concentration only with the greatest difficulty,
especially under the conditions of a secular life. In order to
delve into themselves—in prayer, in gathering within themselves all their spiritual powers and abilities to the very depths
of their spirit—many have gone off into the desert, dedicating
their entire lives to this spiritual contest, a contest that demands that the soul be purified from all passions—even the
most insignificant ones—and from all distractions, empty
thoughts and minor temptations. Difficult though this path
may be, no religious person can neglect it. Anyone who loves

[2]In Orthodox theological terminology, the "heart" designates not so much
the focus of the feelings of a person but the personality *per se*, i.e., the focus
of a man's entire life, our "I."

God will want to meet Him not only in the wide-open spaces of the world, but within his soul as well.

If inner unity is a requirement for communion with God, unity with other people is no less required. A separated human person is not a "total man," for men and women were created as a single humanity. For this reason, no one can attain inner unity while remaining divided from others. Each of us has only a partial perception of God. The fulness of communion with God is accessible to us only in the unity of all, and then, each person is united with God through all. But, most importantly, where there is division, God is definitely not present. He who abides in love abides in God, not only because he becomes like God—Whose very life is love—but also because love, like any force of unification, is from God.

God is the beginning of unity for all that exists, because He alone is completely Himself within Himself. The full richness of His being is unified within Himself in a certain identity, but in such a way that nothing in this identity loses its own particularity. God is one because there is no other god. He is one because everything in Him is unique: there is but one Father, one Son and one Holy Spirit; one goodness, one truth and one beauty in God. God is one because oneness is the basis of being. The closer we are to perceiving the indivisible unity of God, the closer we come to God and the closer we come to the ultimate apex of being to which all of creation is converging.

V

God is not only unity—He is also fulness of being. When man seeks life's riches he instinctively seeks for God. Even material riches involuntarily summon forth in the soul of a religious person the idea of Providence. The infinite diversity of being in the universe likewise turns us toward God. In religious life we seek the spiritual strength that will sanctify the whole of our existence and make it productive. Upon everything that is not evil lies the stamp of the divine image, yet God cannot be equated with the universe in its unity, as the pantheists think: He is the fulness of all goodness, of all the positive properties and modes of being in existence, yet as the Creator He eternally embraces all of creation in His love and in His thoughts. Having created the world, He fills it with His own presence.

If God is the fulness of all goodness, then it is clear that only in God can all of man's aspirations find fulfilment, and man becomes willing to give up his life in order to some day be in God. When man rejects or forgets God he immediately makes himself, or the world, or animals, or society, science or art, into a god. We must understand that this is the greatest, most destructive self-deception. We can be gods in union with God, but when separated from God we are insignificant, powerless and evil. All the grandeur and magnificence of the world is but a senseless mass of matter if there is no God. Animal life by itself can never satisfy man; once we have taken our fill of delight in it we turn upon it with our spirit's full, passionate force: we violate it and destroy it. Animals are beautiful, but the man-animal is an abomination. Society, when idolized, is a horrible monster which devours people— it devastates and torments man. Science, when it is idolized, is a false idol, for it has never and will never possess either omniscience or infallibility. On the contrary, nothing is easier than to exploit science for the sake of falsehood and the destruction of the world. Art, when it has become an idol, degenerates into ambiguous fantasy or the pursuit of original, striking forms.

Society cannot exist without God, for it must be rooted in goodness, and goodness is God. Science and art are nourished by truth and beauty, but absolute truth and beauty are God. An alternative path is, of course, skepticism—the denial of all that is absolute and perfect. But then man takes arms against his own spirit and brings it to extinction, for in his desires, his knowledge, his feelings, in goodness, in truth and in beauty man always seeks for fulness. In God we lose nothing—not even the most minute value of the created world—but rather we gain in addition that which cannot be found anywhere in the universe.

VI

If God is Spirit, He is a person, for an impersonal spirit is an invention of philosophers. An impersonal essence or reason, or an impersonal law ruling the world, is not only unthinkable, but, were it to exist, it would rather be terrifying to us, for it would be a bound, unconscious power, subjected to impersonal necessity. However, God is freedom, consciousness and goodness. His relations with everything are personal, full of condescension and readiness to take into consideration each and every peculiarity of our lives. God's wisdom is free, creative and good, and His truth is that of a father for his children rather than that of a dead law that knows no mercy. And our relations with God ought to be deeply personal, the relations of children with their father or of a man with his friend.

Such a relationship is most simply expressed in prayer. Prayer is turning to God not only with requests, thanksgiving and glorification. The most important element in prayer is standing before God as before a living person; it is living communion with Him. Precisely for this reason is prayer one of the principal paths to God. Prayer is an unerring measure of our religiosity: if God is foreign to us, if our soul is self-satisfied, absentminded, seized with cares, passions, irritations and animosity, it is virtually impossible for us to pray. The deepening of prayer is a long path of deepening and cleansing the soul and of reviving our faith, but along this path there awaits us an encounter with God, conversation with Him, comprehension of Him and of His will for us. Prayer ought to be continual, it ought to embrace our entire life, which would thus be brought before the face of God. Prayer is tormenting work, for everything that is evil within us rises up against it, but prayer is a great strength and joy. If communion with other people can strengthen, renew and comfort us, what then can be said of communion with God? Our prayer is especially strong and pleasing to God when it is common prayer, "with one heart and with one mouth," shared with other people.

VII

The material and organic world is not a world of thought. Only man can think, knowing himself and everything that surrounds him. In our mind an entire ideal world is borne in which is reflected everything we know. But we see that the universe is filled with wisdom, that in acquiring the knowledge of the truth we do not invent it but perceive it through our spiritual eyes. The truth about the universe is neither matter nor a human concept.

What is the source of this truth and this wisdom, which penetrates all that exists without merging with it, this wisdom which abides in the world but is not the world itself? Philosophers have invented an ideal world or a world soul having, as it were, an independent existence. But everything that is spiritual is personal, and the universe is not a single, living being, such that it could have a soul. The world of thoughts and ideas must belong to someone's mind. Whose thoughts, then, fill the universe? It is obvious that only an absolute being could conceive of all that exists and of all that has ever existed. Every thought or idea of God is the eternal plan for something that in fact exists. In accordance with these plans God has created everything in the universe, and His creative thought continues to communicate meaningful, unbroken existence to everything. God's powers and actions are always meaningful and His thoughts always efficacious. It is precisely in the divine ideas that we find an ideal measure of the truth toward which we are striving when we try to know anything.

All truth reveals to us not only what is, but what ought to be as well, for reality itself would be incomprehensible for us without this. If we do not know how things ought to be, how then can we distinguish good from evil, health from disease, beauty from ugliness, etc.? The wisdom of God is the wisdom of the world. It ought to become our wisdom as well. Inasmuch as creation is similar to God, and inasmuch as the basis for the existence of all creation lies in God, then if we know the world (and the spiritual world in particular) we already know God. From this point of view God appears to us as the Idea of all ideas, as the prototype of all that exists, as the Creator and Sustainer. Such knowledge of God is already extremely rich, because it encompasses the concept of God as perfect Being. Can we know God as He is in and of Himself? True knowledge is contemplation that is directly experienced, and we are unable to achieve contemplation of God in the inner depths of His being. However, God reveals Himself to us, and we can deepen our contemplation of Him by involving the effort of our entire life.

God is spirit, and all of our images and words are powerless to express his spiritual nature. Therefore, all literary knowledge about God is only conditional. Our mind has to ascend through what the words express toward God Himself. We must not allow ourselves to be imprisoned by abstract and literary knowledge. Contemplation of God is possible, but the path to this lies, of course, not only through our whole spiritual life, but especially through faith in that doctrine of God which is given to us in the Scriptures and the tradition of the Church. This doctrine ought to bring us not only to a rational interpretation of itself, but also to communion with God, in which those things that we have taken and conceptualized will become actual divine reality. Every word of divine revelation—just as everything in the world—can be a window through which we can see God, even if this be only in one of the forms of His Being. God is truth because He knows Himself wholly, because He possesses perfect, true being and because from Him proceed and by Him are measured all truths.

That which we have said concerning wisdom as a path to God can also be applied to beauty. The beauty of the external world and the inner beauty of man lead us to the ideal beauty in which we see the prototypes of all creation as they exist in God, for God put not only wisdom into the world, but beauty as well. It is precisely in these ideal, divine prototypes of beauty that we must seek the true measure of the beauty of everything human, earthly and heavenly. But God is beauty itself, for He is living harmony; the whole of the divine life is permeated with ideal measure, harmony and peace. In order to attain the divine beauty we too must follow the path of spiritual measure, harmony and peace. The Scriptures and all religious art (the worship services, the rituals, the icons, the church buildings) reveal to us in an external way something of the divine beauty. It is up to us to ascend from these images to the prototypes of the beautiful.

VIII

The truth is also the ideal and law of life. God is truth because He lives in the truth. The moral path to God is an exceedingly obvious one: perfection in our life ought to lead us to the One Who is perfect life itself. In morality we conform ourselves to God, and God is the ultimate focus of our moral life. In His presence we ought above all to be humble; we ought to love Him more than we love anyone else. In Him we find true peace, and we must serve Him. In all positive virtues (i.e., those that are more than simply restraining from evil, such as humility, love, peace and good deeds) there is an expression of the truth of the divine existence. In general, all the laws of universal existence—both the spiritual and the material alike—originate in God, and in the light of them we can judge what God is in the same way that we judge what He is in the light of the wisdom and beauty of creation. God is the lawgiver and the judge. He judges not only directly, face-to-face—as at our personal judgment after death or at the end of the world—He also judges secretly through the inward action of His laws. All misfortunes— spiritual, mental and physical—to which we are subject as a result of sin, are a manifestation of our violation of the divinely established laws. The fundamental principles of all laws of existence are the principles of unity in diversity and of perfection. God desires that not only in Himself, but everywhere (inasmuch as this is possible) there be fulness of existence in unity and harmony, and in striving for perfection.

IX

We have seen more than once that God is the all-perfect Being Who transcends the created world and is even inaccessible to it by reason of His infinite superiority over it, and at the same time, He is the Being Who in Himself embraces the universe and condescends to each creature. Why is it that being absolute Spirit and absolute good, God does not limit Himself to His absoluteness, that He does not live within His own person alone? The answer to this is simple, but extremely important if we are to understand the whole of Christianity. For God, any positive existence is valuable, no matter how small and relatively imperfect it may be.[3] All the more valuable to Him is that existence which is equal to Him or approximates His perfection. If any good is valuable for God, then He obviously loves it, for love is nothing other than the will that that which is loved should both exist and that it should enjoy all good things that are accessible to it. Furthermore, love is a striving for a life lived in union with the one who is loved, a striving to give oneself to the one who is loved and to possess him. Therefore, love gives birth. Love produces, creates, does good, seeks to be united with the one who is loved into a single being; love seeks to live by him, in him and for him. It is important to note that love itself seeks to give existence to the one who is loved, and not merely to love that which already exists, for love impels the one who loves to come out of himself and to live no more by himself alone. Therefore, love multiplies that which it can love.

God loves Himself; He accepts His own existence as a positive reality. But He also loves all good and gives existence to everything. The divine love has three essentially different expressions: it is realized (1) in the existence of the Holy Trinity; (2) in the entire world of the divine self-revelation, to which we can become communicants; and finally (3) in the created world. God did not desire to be alone, and there-

---

[3]Negative existence is evil—i.e., from negation, separation, division, destruction, distortion, hatred, pride, etc., come diseases, sufferings and death.

fore in eternity He gave birth to the Son and breathed forth
the Holy Spirit. This Christian doctrine may seem strange,
but in it is found the ultimate wisdom of Christianity. God
is Spirit; therefore He is a person. Can a person be satisfied
with his own existence, even if he possesses all good things
but yet is not accompanied by another person similar to himself? Is fulness of life and blessedness possible in isolation?
We try to express ourselves, to realize all of the richness of
existence that has been given to us, but we are able to do this
only in another person who is similar to ourselves, for everything that is impersonal is inferior to us. What can be higher
in this world for man than another man? Is not everything
great that we do on this earth done in order to be given to
other people? There is no greater blessedness than to give
life to another, to give him the very best, the most cherished
thing we have within ourselves, and to see how he uses it in
life, how he realizes in himself our wisdom, our ideals, all
the richness of our life. Who is there to love in isolation?
With whom is there to be communion? What can be truly
new and original other than a new person? What can enrich
us more than a life in common with others? Thus, the fact
that God is in three persons is not at all strange; on the
contrary, a God being alone would be impoverished and in-
complete. In His Son, God the Father has in a new, personal
image the fulness of His own wisdom, the full content of
His essence. In the Holy Spirit He has in another person the
fulness of His life and His love. God the Father is the initial
cause of all that exists; He is love itself and the first will of
universal existence. From Him has everything proceeded, and
union with Him is the goal of everything. In the Father, the
Son and the Holy Spirit are expressed three most perfect forms
of personal existence, which cannot be reduced to one. Their
communion encompasses the ineffable riches of mutual love.
The Father, the Son and the Holy Spirit are three absolutely
original, free, conscious, loving and creating persons; and at
the same time they are one God, one Being having one
essence, i.e., the same divine perfections and identical content
of their existence—one and the same will, reason, truth, righteousness, beauty, peace, holiness and blessedness.

The inner life of the Holy Trinity is the summit of the divine existence. But in the same way as the sun fills all space with its light, so God reveals the full content of His hidden tripersonal existence in innumerable expressions of His will, in thoughts, in actions and, finally, in His glory. Thus, God exhausts all the possibilities of spiritual existence compatible with His divine dignity. These actions and thoughts of God are related not to the created world alone. God expressed Himself in these actions also without respect to creation. However, it is precisely through these divine manifestations that we come to know God and enter into communion with Him. It is precisely through them that God created the world and provides for it. In the glory of God, the divine perfection is manifested in forms which are perceptible even to our senses (i.e., sight, hearing, touch). Manifestations of the glory of God are always magnificent and mighty; this is the light in which God lives. In His glory, God comes as close as possible to our physical existence, and makes Himself felt by us.

The absolute character of the divine being does not prevent Him from being the Creator. He not only desired to exhaust all possibilities of existence for Himself, but He did this for us as well, because God has created all things, not disregarding the tiniest creature. The divine creation demonstrates once again God's consciousness of the fact that all existence, even perhaps the most insignificant, is valuable and worthy of love. In the creation, providence and salvation of the world we have revealed to us God's supreme humility and love. He descends to everyone and unites all with Himself. Therefore, there is no other path to God for us also than that of humility and love. The more we are aware of how valuable everything in existence is—even a single atom or tiny insect, not to speak of people or worlds, or the Creator of all Himself—the closer we come to God, Who excludes nothing from His own benevolence. The more we love and do good, the more we seek unity of life with all that exists and with God, the closer we will be to God, for He loves all, does good to all and is united with all.

X

To believe in God is natural and not difficult; not to believe in Him is unnatural and unreasonable. But the majority of all religious people limit themselves to an acknowledgment of the existence of God and a more or less virtuous life. Communion with God seems completely inaccessible to most people, even though it is in such communion that the essence of the religious life really lies. The fact is that we are engrossed in worldly life, and the spiritual life frightens us away because we imagine it to be something boring, difficult, quasi-professional and almost hypocritical in an external sense. The spiritual life is not an external form of behavior— it is first of all love for good, truth, righteousness, beauty and, above all, love for God, man and the world, no matter how timid this love may be at first. Anyone who has come to love all of this, anyone who has experienced though only to a small extent that there is love for God and creation, anyone who has the patience step after step to overcome the darkness and heaviness of his own soul—such a person will draw near to God throughout his entire life. If we love only ourselves or simply that which is external and purely human, then communion with God will be impossible and unnecessary for us. If we are fascinated by the life of the Church or of society, by the truth or by art, *not* out of love for God and other people, or for truth and for beauty, but rather for whatever other reasons, then, of course, such fascination cannot in the slightest sense bring us closer to God. In order to live in God, one must participate in the very life of God.

Knowing our fleshliness, our weakness and our corruption, God revealed to us a newer, more accessible, although unconventional path of union with Him: through His Son Who became man, and through His Spirit Whom He sent into the Church.

XI

In Christ, God came down to earth and appeared to us as a man. Therefore, anyone who knows Christ knows God; anyone who loves Christ loves God; anyone who lives by Christ lives by God. It is amazing how little Christians value this tremendous possibility of union with God through man. We have but to gaze attentively at the image of Christ and the image of God will appear to us, feature by feature. Christ is filled with the forces of life: He performs miracles, He heals, He raises the dead and Himself arises, He has dominion over nature, He manifests the divine glory, He heals from sin, He transfigures the whole man, communicating to him eternal life in spirit and in truth and giving him the very powers that He Himself possesses, for God is Life. Christ unites in Himself the entire universe with God, for God is unity. Christ is a living person who lives in the fulness of freedom and consciousness, for God is a personal Being. Christ is humility itself, for God is full of humility and condescension toward all. Christ's entire life is love, for God is love. Both Christ's life and His doctrine are truth, for God is truth. Christ was the most beautiful of all people, for God is beauty. Christ believed His entire life was to show the power of the spirit rather than of the flesh, for God is Spirit and in Him external might is secondary. We speak here not about simple similarity, but about how in Christ the divinity penetrates and defines everything human.[4]

When we live by Christ, we live by God, for Christ is God, and it is sufficient that we live by Christ's humanity in order also to live by His divinity. But how can we be in communion with Christ? Christ Himself established two sacramental means of union with Himself: baptism and the eucharist. In baptism, Christ abides in us and we are born as Christians; it is as though a certain invisible seed of the life of Christ is planted in our soul. In the eucharist we receive the body and blood of Christ and through them enter into

[4]We speak here about our Lord Jesus Christ only briefly, as a separate article was already dedicated to Him. See above, pp. 21-61.

communion with Christ and partake of the great victory of the cross and of His spiritual body, the Church. The sacraments give us the gift of a special presence of God, but every one of God's gifts requires assimilation on our part, otherwise it will remain in us as the talent hidden in the earth.

In what should our effort for assimilation consist? First, we must have faith in Christ, but this should not be limited to a simple confession of the fact of Christ's existence as God and man. The image of Christ should be always present in us in as full a way as possible, and everything that relates to Christ should be for us just as real as our own being. The image of Christ is given to us in the New Testament. Reading and rereading it should first of all engrave upon our soul all that is said about the life of Christ. Secondly, it should bring us to understand the doctrine of Christ and of His apostles, for the apostles' doctrine either coincides in full with Christ's own, or explains and expands upon it. Christ's doctrine is Christ Himself in His word; and His word, when we have applied it to our lives, possesses transfiguring grace and power. Christ lived as He taught others to live. Both Christ's earthly life and His doctrine stem in like manner from the truth whereby He lived and was. Anyone who has in himself the image of Christ and His doctrine lives in the light and can commune with Christ if he will only love Him and live like Him. Anyone who loves Christ will want to belong to Him and live a life in common with Him. Remembering Christ constantly, we will turn our thoughts and feelings to Him and seek personal communion with Him—first of all, perhaps, in simple prayer to Him, later in prayerful conversation with Him and inner awareness of His actual presence in us. When we sense the presence of Christ we will see Him in everything that is good in the world, for Christ is God, the Wisdom of God by Whom all things were created and exist. All truth is a manifestation of Christ.

Many people strangely err, thinking that they can be in union with Christ and God without living in conformity to Christ. Even two men cannot live together if they live in completely different ways. And love is precisely life in common. How can we be united with Christ if our entire life is outside Christ? On the contrary, to live in a Christian way must mean to be close to Christ.

XII

Christ came in order to unite us with God through His own humanity, yet we manage to find in this an excuse for our inability to follow Christ. Our main excuse is our weakness—sins and cares have such mastery over us, we are so fainthearted that we are unable to draw near even to the man Christ, let alone to the invisible God. But God foresaw this and gave us the means to overcome even this obstacle by sending us the Holy Spirit. The manifestation of the Spirit of God is, first of all, the action of His grace. In His grace, the Holy Spirit is actively present in us. Forms of His gracious action are just as numerous as our life is diverse. Grace strengthens our will, multiplies our faith, enlightens our mind, inspires our senses, helps us complete any good work, extinguishes our gusts of passion, heals the diseases and perversions of our bodies and souls, comforts us in our sufferings, leads us to Christ and brings us to God. Grace can act imperceptibly, or it can seize us with such force that we feel overwhelmed by the Spirit of God. How can we receive the gifts of grace? We receive them through the sacraments (especially through chrismation), and through everything that unites us with God: through faith and truth, through love and all good. God demands on our part a firm resolution for good and prayer. If we waver in our resolution we cannot be helped—just as one cannot help someone walk who does not want to stand. Our prayer is necessary for God to aid us only because it opens our soul to Him and makes communion with us possible for Him.

The first sign of grace is the presence within us of powers that transcend our own powers; we sense that our actions and experiences contain something greater than that of which we ourselves are capable. Grace inspires and warms our soul. It is the light by which we see the truth clearly and discern good from evil. It is the joy of divine life in freedom and power. It is the love of God which awakens love in us. It is the fire which purifies and vivifies us, and we can transmit this fire to others. Grace transfigures us from within according to the image of Christ; it unites us with Christ and gives us the power to live in a Christian way. We must remember that the Holy Spirit perfects only that which conforms to Christ and leads to Him, for He is the Spirit of Christ. Any inspiration that is foreign to Christ is not from the Holy Spirit. We are born of the Spirit in baptism, and we live by His grace. The Holy Spirit gives life not only to us, but to the entire universe as well. Everything that has existence has the Holy Spirit. But our relationship with the Holy Spirit should not consist solely in seeking to live by His power. The Holy Spirit is a living person, just as Christ, the Son of God is. His image, too, is revealed to us distinctly in the Scriptures, and we must conform ourselves to His divine features. It is natural for us to seek personal communion with the Spirit. In Him we encounter the life of God in its personal image. He is the Spirit of Holiness, the Spirit of truth and beauty, the Spirit of peace and the joy of God. The movement of the Spirit of God is flaming and quiet and meek in His very omnipotence. Together with Christ He intercedes for us before the Father with groanings which cannot be uttered.

XIII

Thus, God sends His Son and His Spirit in order to bring us to Himself. The final goal of the incarnation of the Son and the manifestation of the Spirit lies in unifying us with God the Father, in order that we might become children of God. To be a son means to proceed from the father, to be in conformity with him and to have his nature. To be a son means to be loved by the father and to be under his protection, and to love the father and to serve him. We proceed from God the Father on the very basis of the fact that He is

our Creator, but we Christians also proceed from Him in a
special sense inasmuch as we live by the life of His Son and
His Spirit. Living in Christ by the grace of the Holy Spirit,
we participate in the divine nature.

All people are like God, but evil has to a large extent
distorted our likeness to God. Christ, Who was Himself the
eternal image of God, restored within Himself the true image
of man. In Him we too once again become like God. God the
Father loved us eternally; for this reason only did He create
us and not give us over once and for all to perish in wickedness. But God's love for the sinner is hampered by his sin.
The sinner rejects the love of God, he needs God only to
ask Him for external benefits. The sinner either fears God
or rejects Him. But insofar as we live in Christ we are wholly
open to the love of God and pursue good—not like wicked
servants, but because we want to be like God, and nothing can
separate us from the love of the Father. Every Christian is
under God's special protection and can ask God for anything
with boldness. Only our lack of faith and faintheartedness
deprive us of God's protection. If we live by God, neither
trials nor death will be terrible for us, for in God we already
have eternal life. Christians are free from the powers of this
world precisely because they depend upon God and not upon
the world, and they know that without the will of God not
a single hair will fall from their heads. Confidence in the
omnipotence of God's love and truth frees us from slavery
to the world and the horrors of life. If we are children of
God we belong to Him and live by fulfilling His will, just as
Christ did, Who on earth completed the work of God which
the Father had entrusted to Him, including the acceptance of
the cross. The Christian is not merely inwardly immersed in
the divine life: he ought in all things to be a servant of God.
We ought to fulfil God's commandments, to be His representatives on earth, to ponder the path of Providence and set
our strength toward being co-workers with God in realizing
the goals that God sets before us at any given time.

The Son of God and the Holy Spirit are not only inter-
mediaries between God and man. From all eternity, God is
in and of Himself a Trinity, a unity of three co-divine persons.

For us Christians, communion with the life of the Holy Trinity is ultimate blessedness, for it is communion with the fulness of life and love of the Three Who are perfect: the Father of all that exists, His Son Who is truth and His Spirit of life.

XIV

The path to God is the path from the external to the internal, from the spiritual to the divine. In God we find all of the highest good things toward which our soul strives, in their absolute perfection. But above all else is our communion with the Holy Trinity. From the time that the Son of God became of one essence with us men and we began to be born spiritually from the Holy Spirit, God has been our Father, our Brother and our Mother—and this is the goal of our life. But does communion with God impart anything to earthly life? We have already shown that true goodness, truth and beauty come only from God; hence, all moral, cultural and social life will inevitably be false and pernicious if it is not connected with God, who is the perfect foundation of all spiritual values.

God is the Creator of the material world also. In His power lies everything that does not depend exclusively upon our freedom. Therefore, it is false to think that our external life can be independent of God. Man's entire destiny is in the hand of God. At the same time, the external life both of each individual and of entire nations depends upon their inner life. Hence, the religious principle must be the foundation, the focus and the completion of the whole human life. Neglecting the religious life shows lack of judgment, all the more so because God remains our Creator and our Master, even though we deny Him.

XV

Let us turn now to the second side of Christianity, to the

unity of men in God. Christianity professes the irreplaceable value of each human person, as the highest value of the personal form of existence in general. Only a person can be spiritual, only a person can possess inimitable distinctiveness, can be the source of new life, a new creation, the source of love and the bearer of happiness. So great is the value of each person that God creates even those who will become evil. However, the individual value of each human being in no way precludes the general unity of all mankind. People are one by origin and nature. A multitude of bonds exist among them: historical, ideological, cultural, national, familial, political, industrial, etc. Within each of our spirits live all of those with whom we have relations. Spiritually we are united so deeply that this unity does not depend on our will. It is not an accident that alienation from people—or even worse, hatred for others—destroys man inwardly. Isolation is devastation. In each person with whom we come in contact we find an entire new world, a new possibility for love and mutual enrichment. In each of us we find a potentiality for everything, but none of us can realize everything. Each of us has his own special, personal gift, his own special purpose, and this purpose is always connected with our relations with other people. Only in unity and cooperation can we put together something which is really whole; only a life lived in common is real life. Every society, and humanity as a whole, is as it were a single being encompassing many persons.

People can be bound by some single thing: work, a profession, a common interest in something, a common ideal or task. In such a case the value of their unity is directly proportional to the value of that which unites them; in this case there always remains considerable one-sidedness. Society can unite people in many ways, almost totally, as we see in the unity of the family or nation. Unity in the family or nation is, of course, positive in and of itself, but it is very important that we note that the content of family or national life can be extremely diverse: it can be poor or rich, good or bad. If we consider that everything by which our family or nation lives is wonderful simply because it is *our* family or nation, we fall into idolatry.

Christianity does not deny the value of any unity among people that is at least in some way positive, but it recognizes that the highest value of relations among people lies where they are based upon the love of one person for another simply because he *is* a human being. To be a human being is sufficient basis for being loved, and there is no rationale for loving, for example, only a person's talent, or some single characteristic, or class, or nationality, rather than everything that is positive in him. If we were to love all people as people, our love would ultimately spread to all humanity, and it is to this that Christianity call us.

However, no single person nor all people together are self-sufficient beings. Striving for perfection immediately brings man beyond the limits of his nature, for by nature we are limited and have no foundation within ourselves. If people are united only by that which is purely human, the content of their unity is limited and unstable. If we measure goodness, truth, beauty and all good things in general by man's measurement, everything will be superficial and subject to doubt and will depend upon the whim of each of us. If ideals are forced on us by entire parties and governments, they will not be any more true or convincing because of it. Therefore, the true unity of mankind is unity in God, for God can be the focus, the ideal and the measure of everything positive that is capable of uniting us. Whether we be united on the path of love or morality, knowledge or beauty, ideals or creativity, the summit of our path will be in God: in Him all of our highest aspirations converge. Only a common, living love for the only living God, only a common faith in absolute good, truth and beauty can completely unite all people in a single, comprehensive ideal of human life. God also is the perfect power of unity, for He is love. Love unites in itself all who exist, and it gives existence to those who as yet do not exist, in order to unite them also in a single life. The love of God, just like human love, multiplies humanity and unites all into one.

XVI

Men have lost God and therefore have lost their unity. Thus, Christ was sent by God to once again unite all. Christ was one of us men, but in His Spirit as the God-man He united all men and revealed to them God, the perfect ideal of man, the one truth and the truth for all mankind. Christ restored in man his very aspiration for God and for everything exalted; He restored the love for God and for one's neighbors and brought divine love down to earth. Therefore, Christ became the unifier and the reconciler for all. Because Christ took upon Himself the sins of all, we, therefore, cannot condemn anyone in Christ. The Spirit of God is the Spirit of love; through His innumerable gifts He leads all men to God. Wherever there is disunity, neither God nor Christ nor the Spirit is to be found. Christ and the Holy Spirit lead us to the one God for Whom we are all one and equal. The unity of the Holy Trinity is both the ideal and the power of our own unity. It is the ideal because we all ought to strive to form a single being, to live by one content of goodness, truth and beauty, while at the same time preserving the full individuality of each of our persons, just as the Father, the Son and the Holy Spirit have a single essence and are a single Being. The Holy Trinity is also the power of unity since through Christ and the Holy Spirit we are united as children of the divine Father into a single divine-human family.

The unity of men in Christ is the Church, the family of God, the Kingdom of God or the body of Christ. Unity is the essence of the Church. In the Church all is one, although it remains diverse.

XVII

How easy unity would be if only evil did not divide people, if only we did not quarrel and become loathsome to each other in our wickedness! The path of unity is a long one. It begins with humility, i.e., the recognition of the unconditional value of all human beings regardless of how insignificant or evil they may seem to us to be. It is not difficult in good will to wish everyone well and show compassion, nor is it so difficult to rejoice in another's good fortune. It is difficult, however, to progress from outward relations with others to inward ones, for this is connected with our common superficiality. One must learn to penetrate inside everything and to comprehend the value of the spirit and its power. The deeper our relations with others are, the more we will be attracted to them. It is possible for us to live a life in common with other people, though at first with only a few. For believers this is natural and necessary. There is no sadder picture than the disintegration of a church community. If at present the close unity of millions of believers is unthinkable, all those for whom Christianity contains the whole meaning of life ought to have as their immediate goal the formation of at least small groups of Christians who are truly united in faith and in love. Such groups united among themselves would be the leaven of a general unity and renewal.

Christ took unto Himself all of us sinners; He redeemed us all and transfigured us in Himself. Therefore, in Him is the ideal image of each person, and Christ Himself abides in each of us. When evil causes us to hate a person, let us humble ourselves before the humility of Christ, Who does not shun that person but rather awaits his salvation. The goal of the Christian is to rescue others from evil. If we are powerless to do this (often this is the case because we ourselves are evil), then we must be patient. Perfect love casts out fear not only of God, but of evil as well, for love believes in the victory of good over evil, when evil has not been completely consolidated through conscious choice. The person who loves sees good, and he knows that everything good is already united in Christ, in the Kingdom of God, and that evil has power only over those who of their own free will have doomed themselves to spiritual death by their hatred for God, other people and everything that is good. Through love of Christ we belong not to this evil world but to the Kingdom of God, which exists already here on earth, although it is not evident to all. Christ gathers and will gather all into a single Kingdom.

XVIII

If the unity of all people is founded in God and in Christ, then it is understandable why in the Church such great importance is given to the saints and the angels, who so obviously belong to the Kingdom of God. The saints are opened to us because they live by love; they unite us with Christ because Christ is in them. Communion with the saints should not be limited to their veneration; there should be true communion in which we are able to be enriched by their sanctity and wisdom and share the joy of their perfect life.

To the extent that we live in Christ we are all saints. Following Christ and being inspired by His Spirit, we cannot sin. If we subordinate our will to faith, if we live as members of the Kingdom of Christ, we are animated by good and can do only good. To the extent that we are evil and do evil, we are not in Christ and do not belong to His Kingdom. It is tremendously important that we understand that in his earthly life each Christian belongs simultaneously to Christ and His Kingdom, on the one hand, and to this world and all the evil pertaining to it, on the other. The main point is this: to which does our heart belong? We can sin through weakness even though from the depths of our soul we are turned toward God; and we can dedicate our heart to the world and give to God only the leftovers of our soul and life. Of course, within many of us there is a constant battle between God and the temptations of this world, which prevents us from deciding which is the most important to us. Such a state cannot go on forever; at some point we must make a choice. In our personal lives and in the life of the Church we must learn to strictly distinguish that which is truly Christian, i.e., that which is founded in Christ, from that which is not only obviously evil, but also simply worldly, of a spiritually doubtful character. Both Christians and non-Christians often confuse Christianity with that which only uses its name as a cover.

If in Christ it is impossible to sin, it is also impossible in Christ to lie or go astray. If we sincerely and wholly dedicate our mind to Christ, praying that He will illumine us by His

Spirit, we will be in communion with the truth. That is the reason why the Church does not err in saying that her mind is the mind of Christ. The Church seeks not her own wisdom but wisdom from God in Christ. We err when we dedicate our mind to worldly wisdom, without verifying it by the divine measure. And we all invariably make mistakes inasmuch as we belong to this sinful world. Therefore, the exercise of the strictest possible judgment of truth over all of our knowledge and convictions is absolutely indispensable.

The fulness of holiness belongs to Christ alone. The righteousness of each individual Christian realizes but one of the possible forms of holiness. Hence, there are various ranks of saints: apostles, prophets, martyrs, fathers (i.e., holy theologians), hierarchs (holy bishops), the venerable holy monks, healers, unmercenaries, holy princes, etc. Only the entire assembly of the saints is equal in sanctity with Christ. Similarly, the fulness of authority is revealed to Christ alone, for He is the God-man. Each Christian knows the truth from a certain angle, even though the truth stands fully before him in Christ. But to the unity of all, the truth is revealed in its fulness. The same can be said about beauty. We must not forget that in the perfect combination of unity and multiplicity, originality and identity, we find the basis of good and truth and beauty and of existence itself, for God too is a perfect triunity.

XIX

At the beginning of this article we mentioned that Christianity calls man to unity not only with God and other people, but with the world as well. In this case, we understand by "the world" the material, vegetable and animal world. Our usual relation to it is one of vicious exploitation; modern man is rapidly and universally destroying nature and earnestly studying it in order to exploit it. Occasionally we recognize our error and set up nature reserves, parks, zoological gardens, etc.; we take vacations and enjoy nature. But on the whole it is difficult to expect that man's relationship with nature will change radically before the end of history. Man must be an exploiter of nature and an animal-killer in order to defend his own existence. In particular, if we were today to stop killing animals we would be destroyed by them, probably within a hundred years. From the Christian point of view, this destructive battle with nature is the result of the general fall. Nevertheless, even in our fallen world people could strive to abuse and kill animals and to destroy nature as little as possible. The ideal is not battle, but love for nature.

How is this love justified? In the first place, man himself belongs to nature: each of us is an animal, an organism, a material thing. Hence, nature has an affinity with us, and we are united with it by the very fact of our existence. In the second place, our body and material environment provide us with an enormous opportunity for creativity. All human culture, and especially art, is connected with matter (for example, with sounds, colors, materials). We can be easily convinced that matter and the body possess an absolutely amazing ability to express the finest and most profound spiritual manifestations and experiences; one need only recall music. In the third place, nature itself (as we have said many times already) is filled with wisdom and beauty and, moreover, with the divine presence. Nature is the great book of the divine revelation and the great temple of God. In the world we learn to know God; in the world we can meet God. God loves not only mankind but the whole universe, the whole of creation as well. According to God's plan, man ought to be nature's good master and its organizer in cooperation with the angels who fill heaven and earth. We are the older brothers of all of creation, and of the animals in particular, who in this fallen world are so touchingly faithful to man. The great saints were friends of nature, and the Church lovingly sanctifies it. Communion with nature is a necessity for our life—without it we become dry, abnormal beings in our mechanical and fantastic urban civilization. However, it is only in the distant perspective of the transfiguration of the universe that we can hope for the union of the whole of creation with men and with God.

XX

Why is the inner unity of humanity and the world inseparable from their union with God? We have already said enough about the dependence of people and the world upon God, but it is also clear that God is inseparable from the world. He united Himself with us, wishing to become our Creator, our Provider and our Savior. He Who is perfect Spirit is also the Creator of the universe. We must not divide God. Therefore it is incorrect to separate our relations with God from our relations with the creation in our religious life. Anyone who loves God must also love his brother, because God loves him.

Why do we speak so incessantly about goodness, truth and beauty? Do we not have a certain abstractness here? But the whole indispensable and necessary value of goodness, truth and beauty consists in the fact that we are united in them with reality itself, i.e., with God, men and the world. Indeed, goodness is nothing other than life in truth and righteousness. But the essence of truth and righteousness for Christianity is love; hence, goodness in essence is love and everything necessarily connected with love (humility, doing good, peace, holiness, etc.). Love is not abstractness, but the foundation of life. It gives life; it unites us with everything that is living and with all that is good. It is precisely in love that universal unity is realized.

Truth can be imagined as the fruit of abstract knowledge, but such a view is erroneous. Abstract knowledge is knowledge over-simplified: the scholar who sets for himself a given object of knowledge frees himself from having to think about reality in its fulness; he replaces it with conditional schemata. But truth is not human thought; it is that which really exists and which is revealed to knowledge. Therefore, the truth is God and Christ, and there is truth in everything that exists. Spiritual communion is impossible outside of the knowledge of truth: if I do not know God, mankind, the world—or if I have a false knowledge of them—how can I be in communion with them? On the other hand, if I am one spiritually with God and other people, then by this I know them. Truth is virtually the essence of the spiritual life, because in it we encounter all that exists. Truth binds all because it is one for all.

Beauty likewise is not a conditional creation of our imagination. In it is expressed the very perfection of existence, for perfect existence is harmony, measure, power, the combination of all things in such a way that even the most insignificant is necessary and nothing is superfluous. The perfection of life is revealed to us in beauty more than in anything else. That which is perfect is always beautiful. Hence, in beauty we also enter into communion with reality itself, with God and all that exists. Only fabricated falsification of beauty can be dangerous. One must be delivered from identifying truth with science, or beauty with art. Science and art do not determine truth and beauty; on the contrary, they should be determined by truth and beauty. When we speak of goodness, truth and beauty, we speak not of the artistic work of the human spirit, but about that which reveals to us God and the world and which connects us with them. Therefore, the Kingdom of God cannot but be the Kingdom of goodness, truth and beauty.

Thus, the essence of Christianity is life in the Kingdom of God. The Kingdom of God is the unity of all men in Christ, and in Christ the entire world is united with God. The whole life of man can raise him to God, for God is life. In love, in unity, in wisdom, in truth, in holiness, in beauty, in peace, in all perfections we are united with God, Who is the unity of all perfections. God is a person, and our communion with Him is personal, as is the communion of those who love one another, and as is the communion of a man and wife according to the word of the Scriptures.

The universe is filled with God. He is in our souls; He is among us as man. We are born in God and Christ is born in us. We grow in Christ and are nourished by the word of His truth and by Himself. The power of our life is the Spirit of God, and the Spirit Himself is our life. God is our Father, for by His Spirit we live a life united with His Son. We abide in the Father's love under His almighty protection. We belong to God and serve Him on all the paths of His truth and Providence. The Kingdom of God is the Kingdom of the Holy Trinity. The life of the Trinity is our absolute ideal. Life in the Trinity is our goal and blessedness. The Kingdom of God is God's family. Anyone who turns his heart toward God and Christ belongs to His Kingdom. All who have entered the Kingdom of Christ are brothers of one another. All have one soul and one life. The Kingdom is a single organism no matter how many millions of people enter it. The Kingdom of God is the kingdom of love, for love unites all. It is the kingdom of truth, for in truth God, His truth and the true image of man are revealed. It is the kingdom of peace, for concord and inner quiet reign in it. It is the kingdom of beauty, for its life is perfect. It is the kingdom of joy in God, men and the world in the hope of universal salvation from evil.

The Kingdom of God is in the world, but it proceeds from God and Christ. It does not depend upon the world; the measure of our belonging to it depends solely upon us. No force whatsoever can separate us from God, or from love, or from truth or from any other spiritual good. Only unbelief or insufficient faith, sin or faintheartedness can cause us to renounce the Kingdom of God. Our very destiny in the world depends upon God; therefore, the Christian does not feel as though he is defenseless in the face of evil. He can be free from all influences of the world, from agonizing anxiety and the fear of calamities and destruction. He who abides in the Kingdom of God has even more than this: he believes that Christ's spiritual victory over the world has already been accomplished, because perfect life has been established in Christ for all mankind.

In fact, everything positive already belongs to Christianity, even though this is not universally self-evident. Sooner or later, everything that is good will be gathered into the Church, and at the end of the history of the world the universe will become the Kingdom of God. Evil will fall away into hell; only that which is good will remain with God, Christ and the saints in a transfigured world. Spiritual resurrection is possible for men while still in this world. Spiritually we can already become new creatures and participate in eternal life. In this case, after the physical resurrection at the end of the world we will enter the new world totally transformed by God. All who were finally confirmed in evil here will be in a separate world of evil, which in theological terminology is called hell. God forces no one to enter His Kingdom. Everyone is free to choose good or evil, but the confusion of good and evil within a single world must cease.

THE CHURCH ON EARTH

XXI

The essence of Christianity and the Church lies in the Kingdom of God. How is it connected with earthly life, and how can we enter it? The Church is established on earth by God, by the power of faith and Christian knowledge, by the power of the sacraments, prayer, ecclesiastical organization, by the power of moral and creative life and by truly Christian relations with the world.

Faith is the beginning of the Christian life. Faith is the perfect conviction of the truth of Christianity on the basis of the Church's witness, a witness which ascends to Christ Himself. The Church knows about Christ through tradition, which comes from the depths of the ages; she knows Him directly as well, by experiencing life in Christ. Faith is not only theoretical knowledge that increases our knowledge—the knowledge of faith is addressed to each of us as a guiding life force. Weak faith consists in the fact that we recognize truth as a general principle but are afraid to apply it to ourselves. True knowledge is based on personal experience, but our personal experience is always limited. Ninety percent of our knowledge is based on trust in other men or scholars. We cannot have religious experience until we begin to live a religious life, and we cannot have a religious life until we believe in God. From the very beginning we can pose two questions. First, how reliable are the New Testament and the experience of the saints and teachers of the Church, who in their personal lives practiced Christianity? And second, does Christianity make sense? Is it not full of contradictions and foolishness? There is no basis for us to reject the historical witness of the New Testament to Christ, and the lives of the saints show that no one who has lived in a truly Christian way has become disillusioned in it. Furthermore, in Christianity there are no contradictions; we can be convinced of the sensibility of any Christian concept if we will only carefully study its real meaning.

Must the Christian always accept Christian doctrine only on faith? If we live in a Christian way, if we enter deeper into the meaning of Christianity with our whole soul and mind, our faith will gradually become knowledge: experience and contemplation confirm what has been accepted on faith, and our meditations reveal to us the integral meaning of dogma. We believe in order to know. In the Kingdom of God faith becomes knowledge. The spiritual life is a reasonable life; communion with God is impossible without thought. God is Spirit, and a Spirit can be comprehended only by thought. Therefore, eternal life coincides with knowledge of God. Thus, we cannot even be in communion with Christ if we do not come to know His doctrines and life. In general, only in love and in knowledge can we embrace all that exists —God, mankind and the world. Expanding our knowledge is expanding our life. Love itself, in uniting us with the one we love, gives us knowledge about him.

At first we find the content of dogma in books. Every Christian ought to know the Holy Scriptures, for in them are written what God Himself has revealed and what the apostles have told about the life of Christ. Everyone should know the Creed and the principal pronouncements of the ecumenical councils, for in them are expressed the Church's judgments on the most important truths. We ought to know the major ideas of the fathers of the Church, since by them ecclesiastical doctrine is most authoritatively expounded. For the same reason it is important to know the texts of the sacraments and the basic liturgical services. It is necessary to

know Church history as well, as the history of Christian life
and especially of the lives of the saints. However, one must
avoid the danger of self-satisfied and abstract knowledge;
books are given to us in order that through them we might
approach reality itself. We ought to remember that any
thought expressed in words and concepts is always conditional
and limited. It is important to acquire a comprehensive view
of the very object of what we are learning, without isolating
it from everything else in the process. The path of Christian
learning is impossible without prayerful meditation and contemplation.

XXII

Knowledge is the light of life, the power of a Christian
life in grace or, in other words, the active presence within us
of the Spirit of God. Christian life as a whole should be full
of grace and should draw God to us. Without God's direct
cooperation a Christian life is impossible; we are too weak
and spoiled to live in goodness by our own powers. God
awaits our prayers for help. For the most part we just ask for
external things. However, if we were truly resolved to do
good, and if our hearts were directed toward God, much of
what seems inaccessible in our internal and external lives
would become possible for us. Our most accessible source of
grace is in the sacraments, for in them grace is communicated
to us through certain external means—the words of prayer,
rituals, water, bread and wine, chrism, oil and the laying-on
of hands. However, the gracious power of the sacrament is
assimilated in us according to the measure of our faith, our
spiritual purity and true yearning for life in correspondence
with the spirit of the sacrament. Every sacrament has its own
specific, vital goal. In general, Christianity believes in the
possibility of the manifestation of the spiritual and divine in
the material. God is actively present in the material world—
in the body of Christ, in church buildings, in icons, in the
cross, in sacred objects, in ecclesiastical rituals, in the relics

of the saints. Therefore, through them we can touch the divine power. This is not superstition, but the realization of the closest bond between matter and the spirit and the possibility of their mutual penetration.

The significance of the Church's life of prayer and worship is rather obvious. Prayer is a direct path to God; in communal prayer the full power of the unity of the Church is expressed. We know that the Orthodox services, both textually and in their overall structure, are real works of art. Our churches and icons should be the same kinds of creations. In general, Orthodoxy not only invites us to inner beauty, but strives toward beauty of form for the entire life of the Church and of all the faithful. Of course, this external beauty has an inner meaning and impels us to turn toward that which is spiritually beautiful.

XXIII

Organization is necessary for the Church, as it is for any society, but it also has a deeper meaning when we speak of the clergy and of catholicity. The Church arose immediately as a complete society. The clergy belongs to the composition of the Church—it is not called to dominate it as an external power. The Church is a body in which all of the members minister to each other, and leadership in the Church is a ministry. The Lord Jesus Christ, being the head of the Church, is also a member of her and her minister. The Church has a need for someone to be a living center of her life, for one who would look after all aspects of the Church's life, who would be an intermediary between Christ and the flock—not in order to become an obstacle for communication with Christ but to lead people to Him. The clergy's main goal is a spiritual one, to nourish true Christians and to increase their number. For the sake of this goal the clergy is endowed with authority to rule and direct the whole life of the Church, with responsibility for celebrating the services and the sacraments, with the duty of teaching and spiritual guidance and with innumerable pastoral responsibilities; for the bishop or priest, as the father of his flock, must care for its life, must be all things to all people in order to bring all to God and as far as possible must protect them from all evil, including even external evil.

The principle of catholicity in the Church is not simply an expression of equality of rights. Undoubtedly, each Christian bears responsibility for the whole of the Church's life and should take part in it in appropriate ways, according to his own gifts. But in the unity of the whole Church, in its gatherings and councils, are manifested all sides of the great power of that unity by which the Church lives in general. The Church exists in order to unite all in God; only in this unity can we attain the fulness of love, knowledge and authoritativeness which is necessary in order to decide the most responsible matters and problems in the Church. There-fore, Orthodoxy recognizes no greater authority on earth than the ecumenical council.[5] But then the whole life of the Church ought to be a continuous communion among all members of the Church—clergy and laity—in order that everything in the life of the Church would occur in general agreement, coopera-tion and mutual aid. Such a conciliar spirit ought to penetrate the life of every parish, every diocese, every local church and the life of the entire Orthodox world. There are two truths that should never be forgotten in ecclesiastical life: (1) spiritual life—i.e., love for God, mankind and the world, knowledge of truth and beauty—is the main thing; and (2) no human distinctions—sexual, material, professional, educa-tional, social, national or racial—can divide the Church. The unity of the Church is based in Christ, and all Christians, parishes, dioceses or churches should be united, regardless of what differences might be possible among people. Let us not forget that the essence of all existence—from the Holy Trinity on down to the atom, as well as the existence of goodness, truth and beauty—is unity in diversity, i.e., that combination of many into one in which there are no divisions and no loss of each unit's particularity.

[5]The designation "ecumenical" is applied to those councils which were attended by representatives of all the Orthodox Churches.

The Church's activities should not be limited to worship alone. The Church needs schools, publishing houses, educational, youth and charitable organizations, etc. Only violence can deprive the Church of these. It is sad when the Christian community itself does not see the need for Christian culture and a truly Christian social order.

XXIV

If the moral life is humility, love, peace and truth, then its meaning as the path to the Kingdom of God is self-evident. But it is important to note the enormous importance that living love and the preaching of truth have for the Church in her relations with the world. The Church is not called to lock herself within her present boundaries, relating to the rest of the world with indifference or fear. In God's plan the Church is the leaven that must gradually transform the whole world. We should be for the world the source of goodness and truth. The Church can be all of this if only Christians will be inspired by love for humanity, if the destiny of other people will seem as close to them as their own destiny. It stands to reason that a strong and clear faith in the truth of Christianity and its spiritual power is no less important. The majority of Christians do not have a correct and sufficiently broad conception of Christianity.

Faith and love are manifested in deeds. Christianity calls us to love everyone and to do good to all. Faith and love without works are dead and hypocritical. Everyone agrees with this, yet this does not prevent "healthy and sensible egoism" from being almost as widespread among Christians as among all other people of the world. But are Christians called to creativity, to the creation of something original, in which human genius would be reflected? The highest purpose of Christian creativity is the creation of one's own soul and of the souls of others: the creation of the Church. We do not, of course, create a soul in the literal sense, but the most important goal of our life is to remake our soul according to the ideal that we find for ourselves in Christ, and not our own soul alone, but to do likewise for all, to help others also grow into the image of Christ.

This same goal can apply to society as a whole—to create of it a true body of Christ, a society in which Christ would reign. To fulfil this task, the principal task in life for *all* Christians, is unusually difficult. All of our evil, all of our weakness oppose it. We must endure a difficult battle and truly expend all the creative forces of our spirit in order, with the help of God Himself, to see the image of His Son stamped in the very essence of our spirit, or, in a broader sense, the spiritual body of the whole of society. The first task in this spiritual creativity is to see clearly the ideal that we wish to realize. This ideal is given in Christ and given in a special way for each person, for each society. We do not create it, but discerning it demands a deep, pure, intensive faith, a true thirst for the transfiguration of ourselves and others. We can see it only when we understand and experience the essence of Christianity. However, our creative goal is not discerning the ideal but realizing it, no matter how infinitely far we stand away from it. To convert our soul or those of other men, to purify and transfigure them, to raise them to the fulness of life of the Kingdom of God cannot be a matter of mechanical work or scholastic knowledge. Only tremendous effort of the will, mind, artistic sensitivity, continual inspiration and illumination from God can give us success. But the fruit of this creativity is greater than anything else in this world: living persons who have become the precious stones of which the City of God is built. Christ, the prophets and apostles left everything for the sake of this creativity, and both God and the world have glorified them more than all the geniuses of mankind.

From what we have said, of course, it does not follow that Christians should not dedicate their powers to those types of creativity which are usually spoken of in the world, i.e., public service, science, art, etc. These pursuits are justified inasmuch as they serve goodness, truth and beauty and, through them, God and other people. The crucial consideration is whether or not they truly serve them.

XXV

The Church's external life is extremely rich. We have already mentioned ecclesiastical organization, theology, liturgy, ecclesiastical art and the diverse ways in which Christians and the Church act. One can only rejoice over the full richness of the Church's vital activities, and anyone who can introduce something new into all of this richness is worthy of glory. For every Christian, his church activities, his liturgical and theological life are a path to the Kingdom of God and a manifestation of it in the world. However, the experience of centuries of church history and that which we see around ourselves indicate to us that a vast number of Christians visualize these things not as a path but as the very content of the Christian life, thinking that faithful attendance alone, or church activities, or theological knowledge, or a bit of expertise in ecclesiastical art is enough to entitle them to consider themselves true Christians. This is one of the most pernicious delusions in religious society; it is a direct path to hypocrisy, because a semblance of Christianity and the reputation of the churchly person can have no correspondence with true religiosity, which consists in a spiritual life. And the understanding of the spiritual life is constantly oversimplified among Christians to a mere external concentration upon a religious or ascetical life. The apostolic understanding of spirituality is not of this type. Spirituality is abiding in moral purity, love and truth, a life in grace and in Christ.

Very often, the Church as a society is headed by people in whom there is no Christian spirituality,[6] and it is precisely from the example of such people that Christianity is judged. This circle of "churchmen" strenuously supports the viewpoint that people are saved by external piety and obedience, only rarely requiring a certain churchly culture in addition. But the Scribes and Pharisees taught this also. Christian pharisaism is a cruel affront to Christ, who was crucified by

[6]We have in mind here not the clergy *per se,* but in general people who often occupy influential positions in parishes, dioceses, patriarchates, ecclesiastical institutions, etc.

the ancient Pharisees. Let us repeat once more: the essence of Christianity lies in the real union of God and man in Christ, which is equivalent to a life in love and truth. Everything else is only a path to the treasure of the Kingdom of God or its manifestation.

CHRISTIANITY AND THE WORLD

XXVI

What relationship should the Church and every Christian have with the world? Obviously, it should be a Christian one, but unfortunately people often forget this. Some Christians turn away from the world completely, forgetting that it is created by God and inhabited by living people. Others, dedicated to a worldly life, think that in the world it is impossible and unnecessary for one to be a Christian, supposedly because Christianity was created only for ecclesiastical life and not for life in the world, which has its own laws and goals. Such a division is convenient for our weak faith; it preserves our semblance of the Christian life with its hope of eternal salvation and God's help in difficulties, yet it allows us to live in the world in any way we please.

It is correct that the world lies in evil and that it has its own, often evil laws of existence. But at its foundations, the world continues to be God's creation, and every living person, even though poisoned by sin, continues to be valuable to God. Christ came into the world out of love for it and for every sinful soul. Therefore, Christians ought to love the world while at the same time hating its evil and recognizing that it is terribly ill with evil. The Christian should not be carried away by what is worldly, for it is ambiguous and vain. Our life in the world should serve faith and love and be a net drawing the world into the Church. The Christian should be a conscientious worker in all that he does, he should relate with true humanity to all people in all things. He should illumine all things by his Christian consciousness and introduce into everything a Christian spirit. All of this is morally obligatory for all Christians. However, it does not follow from this that all Christians must take part in the usual forms of worldly life by which the majority of people live, i.e., political, domestic, cultural and economic forms. The Church considers renunciation of these forms permissible for those who wish wholly to concentrate upon the inner life, in prayer and spiritual exercises. This is the ideal of monasticism. Of course, even for the monk, love for one's neighbor and the need to help him remain necessary. On the other hand, the Church also blesses those who live by all the forms of the life of the world, as long as these lead to good and not to evil.

XXVII

The Church has never rejected the state. She sees the meaning of the state in the realization of justice and in care for the earthly good of society. But the state can be inspired by both good and evil, and it is limited by the very forms of its activity: it rests upon the power of organization and all the external means of influence, and is essentially unable to engender or determine the spiritual, i.e., the religious, moral, scientific and artistic life which is inspired by God, goodness, truth and beauty, rather than by governmental decrees. The state cannot organize the personal life of men, for there are no laws or general measures that can provide everything necessary for each personal life. In the spiritual and personal life each person must freely choose his own path; in this area the state can but help and encourage, or damage and constrain. The Church should be independent of the state. The administration of the Church can belong only to the Church herself—otherwise she will cease to be herself. Nor are the clergy called to direct the state—they can only judge the state morally and preach the truth. The firm bond between Christianity and the state lies in the Christian citizens of a given country. Even in politics the Christian ought to be a Christian. Christian politics is possible to the extent that politics is connected with questions of human interrelationships, the moral rights and duties of men and their spiritual needs.

It is extremely important to remember that all standards of personal morality also apply to any society. If each person must obey the truth and live in humility, love, truth and peace, then this is also relevant for society. Only the unity of all people, classes, nations and races in truth, in mutual respect, sympathy, agreement and cooperation can be considered the Christian ideal. Egotism, pride, enmity and hatred in all their forms are detestable to Christianity. The future of the whole world and of each nation depends upon our acceptance of this truth. Hatred among classes, among nations, among races, is ready to destroy humanity. No one can deny this self-evident fact. One must remember that to be a human being is infinitely more important than to be a worker or a capitalist, a Russian or an American, white or black; any egotistical and haughty exclusivism within boundaries of whatever kind—personal, class, nationalistic, racial—is pure evil. People will never understand this until they come to understand that the most important thing in man is the spirit, and the human spirit lives by God. God, goodness, truth and beauty cannot be divided on racial, national or class lines. On the other hand, each person and every society has a right to inner freedom, worth and individuality within the confines of the unity of the whole.

XXVIII

Christianity approves of both celibacy and marriage. The meaning of celibacy is the opportunity it brings of dedicating oneself wholly to the service of God and other people. The family constrains a person, though those who are weaker could not live a healthy life without a family, and in most cases the family gives greater strength than it takes away.

God created man male and female. The male and female

types of human being are each in their own way equally valuable and mutually fulfilling. Man and woman each have their own special calling even apart from family life, although it is within marriage that the main purpose of sex is realized. Men and women can have a general human relationship, but if this includes a striving toward exclusive personal unity, the character of such love already becomes sexual in substance. Such love can be realized only in marriage and should lead to it. The whole meaning of love lies in wholeness and uniqueness, in the indissolubility within it of the soul and the body and of all facets of life in general. A husband and wife are one being in all things. Depravity begins when a husband and wife want to possess each other only partially, for only a while, or to share this possession with others. For the most part, in such cases it is a matter of satisfying superficial attraction or fleshly passions. Wholeness is the foundation of purity, and it is possible only within marriage. The task before pastors and teachers is to explain that separating the spiritual from the fleshly in relationships between men and women is unnatural and humiliating, and that the very essence of mutual love between a man and a woman is its exclusivity and wholeness, without which they become beasts and mutilate each other, leaving unfulfilled the essential goal of love—to have another person with whom you are totally united. He who truly loves must always suffer not only from the other's betrayal, but even from the partiality, or more so from the crudeness and selfishness of his love.

The basis of married love lies not in fleshly attraction but in absolute mutual devotion; fleshly union merely fulfils the spiritual. Dissolution of marriage is a crime. The Church advises even widows against second marriage, recalling that loving spouses will meet again in the next world. A second marriage is allowed only through condescension toward weakness. Monogamy, understood not only formally but in its very depths, as the eternal celebration of the total love of a man and a woman united into a single being, is one of the greatest moral ideas of Christianity.

The bearing of children is the crowning of marriage. The love of two people giving life to a new person is beautiful.

All parents know how children bind them together even more closely than before. Relationships between parents and children are not limited to the period of childhood; if the children have received from their parents not only their physical existence but also a spiritual foundation for life, their relationship is eternal. A description of the family is not exhausted by the personal relationships between spouses and their children; it is a unit which is valuable in and of itself. One must love and preserve the family as such. The positions of husband, wife and child have a special substance and a special obligation that transcends personal bonds. The Christian family is a miniature church in which all family relations should be understood in a Christian way.

XXIX

Christianity does not reject science. Knowledge of any sort derives from God. There is but one truth both for theology and for all science. It is false to think that Christianity is true in the religious field while science—even when it attempts to confirm something directly opposite to Christianity—is true in the field of knowledge. Any contradiction between Christianity and any given scientific theory can be resolved by a deeper understanding of theology or by a critical reevaluation of the scientific theory. Scientists too often are mistaken. Human knowledge is limited and unreliable, and it can easily be put to evil use. Therefore, Christianity does not accept any assertion of the scientists without analysis. Science cannot have absolute authority. Natural sciences are relatively objective and reliable, yet much in them turns out to be false and is corrected by later discoveries. But the sciences connected with history, psychology, sociology and with the study of man and human society in general are often, in spite of their enormous development, as doubtful as their theories are bold. The reason for this is obvious: a predominating false and perverted understanding of man. It denies the existence of the soul, of God and of spiritual life; everything is reduced to psychophysiology, to a dark, fleshly subconsciousness. Sociology passes from one extreme of individualism to the other of collectivism (communism, racism, etc.). Christianity, which possesses perfect knowledge of man and of human society and has both a three-thousand-year-old (including the Old Testament) experience of history and foresight as to its final meaning, can give the only sensible basis for the humanities. The link between Christian doctrine and science ought to be Christian philosophy or philosophically structured dogmatics. Unfortunately, we do not as yet have this in the Orthodox world.

Art is beautiful if it serves that which is beautiful. Beauty exists objectively; its basis is God, the divine ideas of the world and Christ as the ideal man. Failure to see beauty signifies blindness, resulting either from nearsightedness or filth. Universal art (not only Christian art) has in the past been a treasury of the beautiful. So-called "modern art"[7] has consciously rejected beauty; it is obtuse and biased when it follows the social order; it is detestable, and at times rank, when it follows sick fantasy and the lifeless orginality of some contemporary creators of art, among whom are hundreds of true talents, but talents that are sacrificed to spiritual nihilism. They plead that nineteenth-century art is outdated and that the contemporary world itself is rotting and dragging with itself art, which portrays what it sees and experiences. We would not call for a repetition of the old; new art is necessary, but the artist ought not to be captive to a dark, putrid reality. He is called to see something greater—that beauty which nothing can destroy in us or in the world, for it is not of us but is essentially coincidental with real being. Life and living things are always beautiful, for behind them is hidden the divine beauty.

Many people perceive Dostoevsky as one of the leaders of modern literature, but this is a misunderstanding. Dostoevsky does not exist without an ideal view of man, and this view is not abandoned even when he writes of murderers or prof-

---

[7]By "modern art" we do not mean twentieth-century art in general, but that "art" which consciously contraposes itself to the ideals and forms of older art.

ligates. People often seek renewal in primitive art, imitating
its forms. But if one were to speak of pagan primitives it
would be strange not to notice their ugliness, convulsed with
fear before the face of mystical evil (idols, masks, etc.), or
simply their dark lasciviousness. We believe that sooner or
later art will return to the eternal source of beauty and will
then find new forms of creativity, rather than wasting talent
on a savage originality.

XXX

Christianity's approach to material life is absolutely unique.
It emphasizes that it is of secondary importance, yet it for-
bids us to neglect it, especially in relation to other people.
Christianity finds the modern mesmerism with wealth and
technical civilization, which is equally characteristic of both
capitalism and communism, profoundly repulsive. At the
same time it is profoundly sympathetic to efforts to destroy
the gloomy poverty that even now grips the majority of
mankind.

Concerning believers, Christianity maintains that they will
never perish from poverty if they will but work with hope in
God. Christianity values any work that is useful for others,
but, of course, it values above all work that brings spiritual
benefit. Poverty is higher than wealth, for by it one is preserved from the temptations of complacency, the exploitation
of others, greediness, stinginess and faith in the supreme
value of money; to be sure, the poor man who spends his
entire life in pursuit of riches is afflicted with the same temptations that are so dangerous to the rich.

With exceptional force, the New Testament summons all
to cooperation. He who has must share with those who lack,
in order that all would have enough to sustain life.

Freedom to work, freedom of economic creativity and free
enterprise correspond to the spirit of Christianity. However,
selfishness, whether on the part of management or labor, is
always repulsive to Christianity. Everything should serve the

common good, i.e., the good of all, and not only an organized collective or the state. Undoubtedly, the spirit of Christianity is compatible both with public control of economic life and the idea of agreement of general economic activity without turning everyone into slaves of the state or of trusts.

Material means ought to serve real needs and spiritual culture rather than luxury, which invariably corrupts people and whole nations, and to which we were witnesses.

CHRISTIANITY AND EVIL

XXXI

Christianity rejoices at all joy not rooted in evil. Thank God for anyone who is happy on earth! May he not fall into self-satisfaction and become oblivious to the fact that next to him there are also those who are unhappy. Let him not believe that his happiness is durable, for nothing on earth is durable. The Christian can achieve true joy and blessedness only in the Kingdom of God. And the whole world is unable to extinguish that joy in God, that joy of new life in love and truth, that joy of unquestionable hope in the coming triumph of truth which will be revealed to the Christian in the Kingdom of God.

However, the world is full of evil. Christianity preaches that the initial cause of evil lies in freedom and in freedom alone. Evil is always primarily an evil act of the will, the meaning of which is negation, isolation, enmity, contempt and hatred. But if evil were only an act of man, it would cease as soon as our will would turn to good. In fact, every evil act leaves a trace in our nature; it perverts and poisons us. We inherit a perverted nature from our parents and ancestors. Furthermore, the very environment in which we live (society, culture, morals) is already permeated with evil. We are born in an evil world, and by our personal sins we increase this evil. To the extent that evil has struck human nature itself, it is a disease, essentially a fatal disease, for man is threatened by evil with both physical and spiritual death. Our inward depravity consists in extreme one-sidedness (e.g., stupidity when our will is strong, intelligence when our will is weak, etc.), in inward contradictions and conflict, in passions which can drive us to obsession, in complexes (i.e., formations within us of, as it were, "bundles" of thoughts, feelings and inclinations from which we cannot separate ourselves and which gradually corrupt and poison our whole soul). In general, any perversion of our life is reflected in our entire being.

At the bottom of evil always lies pride, that is, the sense that one's self is the only thing of value coupled with contempt for others. From pride comes self-love, or concern for oneself alone and subordination of all others to one's own interests. If our pride and selfishness encounter opposition, hatred arises within us, and from hatred comes the urge to destroy and to kill. Of necessity evil is isolation and destruction, murder and suicide, for man cannot live in complete alienation from everyone.

There is still another side to evil, and this is the break in personal relations with God and with other people. Every sin is a sin against God, for all laws of existence are from God. In breaking them we go against God. The vast majority of sins are in one way or another directed also against other people. Hence, every sin makes us guilty before God, before other people and before our own selves, for by them we injure ourselves and others.

The Scriptures teach that evil originally arose in the angelic world and that the devil deceived man. From that time on the kingdom of evil has been the kingdom of the devil; he continually inspires evil in people and, so to speak, organizes and directs it throughout the world. When people commit evil deeds under the influence of some dark force which they do not feel comes from within themselves, that force is the operation of the devil. Without the devil, evil would not be so thoughtless or so unified. Evil is often completely fantastic and quite obviously useless even for human pride and selfishness; at the same time, it is subtly thought out and coordinated with other evil actions, even without the obvious consciousness of the person who commits it.

Christianity confirms a necessary connection between evil, sufferings and death. In our sufferings we experience the same sick perversions that evil introduces into our soul and into our physical life. Death is the final corruption. It is not only the body that sickens and dies, but the soul also; and if the soul is not destroyed, then it is only by the grace of the special will of God preserving its existence even in the presence of evil; but the path of spiritual evil is the path of internal corruption and death.

XXXII

How is the fight against evil possible? The first step is repentance; its beginning is in the confession of one's sins, but its substance is in judging oneself and one's whole life in the light of the image and teachings of Christ, and in the determination to begin a new life in Christ. This new life is not merely a touched-up sinful life, but a genuinely new life based on faith and the power of grace. Deep repentance is an internal self-crucifixion, a renunciation of all that to which we have perhaps become accustomed and that which we have found pleasant, for the simple reason that it is not from God and does not pass the standard of the judgment of Christ. The goal of a Christian is to enter into the Kingdom of God and vigilantly eliminate from one's life all that is contrary to its spirit.

But love of God and mankind, love for truth and good guides us into the fight against evil in human society; it is a gross error to think that only personal evil should disturb the Christian. Indifference to evil in the life of society and the world and in culture is the beginning of weakening and corruption in Christian society. The path of social struggle almost invariably leads to the necessity of sacrifice, sufferings and possibly to death. If we love God and mankind, good and truth, we must be prepared for trials. When our faith is weak, we do not deliver ourselves from sufferings, since our consciences convict us and we break down internally.

The fight against evil limits it, but even if it does not produce fruit immediately, it in any case separates good from evil and demonstrates the power of good, though it be in martyrdom. To the extent that we sense our guiltiness before God and man, our sacrifice for them acquires redemptive significance. We must remember how deep our guilt is and, consequently, how we deserve those sufferings that voluntarily or involuntarily fall to our lot. A man's guilt can only be lifted by total love shown to the offended one and by readiness to make any sacrifice for his sake.

Sufferings and sometimes even death are inescapable in the fight against evil. They have a redemptive quality, but they also have a certain other significance. Sufferings serve to reveal evil. People would long ago have perished from disease and sins if sufferings had not forced us to direct our attention toward external and internal evil, to beware of evil and battle with it. The fear of death likewise often restrains us from evil, although in other cases it drives us to faintheartedness. But, most importantly, death releases from evil those who are subjected to it, as it were, against their will, drawn into evil by the fallen world. For such people death opens up the opportunity for perfect life with God. If there were no death, the fallen state of the world would continue to eternity. But from what we have said in no way does it follow that we should not strive to lessen sufferings or prolong the life of men; this is possible, but only through the fight against evil.

What meaning can the sufferings and death of Christ have for us? First of all they demonstrate their inevitability for mankind. If Christ, who was the perfect man, suffered and died, then there is no way for us to pretend that we will be delivered from sufferings and death. This means that the way of the cross is absolutely unavoidable. Christ suffered for the very same reasons that we also suffer, but he suffered only for us and brought the positive meaning of suffering to its limit. If sufferings serve to warn us against evil, then the sufferings of Christ serve to expose the tragic doom of the fallen world. If sufferings are inescapable in the fight against evil, then the persecutions of Christ demonstrate the complete irreconcilability of good with evil and the impossibility of the victory of evil over good even by means of persecutions. If sufferings, as a sacrifice of love to God and to men, atone for our sins against them, then Christ's sacrifice on the cross, borne by Him in our place in order to demonstrate the perfect love of a man for God, atoned for our sins against God. In Christ all our sins are crucified.

Christianity believes that union with Christ and conformity to His life open a perfect life to us. It likewise believes that internal communion with the sufferings and death of Christ and the taking of the cross upon ourselves for the sake of faith and love is the path of salvation from evil and the path of atonement for our sins. Our voluntary acceptance of the cross unites us with Christ, makes us precious to God, cleanses us and strengthens us in goodness and truth. The path of the cross is the path of wisdom.

Christ accepted our death not with the purpose of atonement alone, but in order to achieve complete triumph over it. Death could not extinguish that principle of divine life which was in Christ: Christ arose, founded the Kingdom of God in heaven and sent down to men the Holy Spirit with the mission to found the Kingdom of God also on the earth. Therefore all those whose souls are now resurrected to life in Christ will be fully resurrected at the end of time unto eternal life. Death for the Christian is passage into the Heavenly Kingdom in expectation of the universal resurrection.

Christ defeated the devil. The devil's support is our sinfulness. The devil is powerless against Christ and against His Kingdom. The Christian does not fear the devil; Christ and the Holy Spirit are our shield against evil. To the extent that we are in the truth, the devil cannot deceive us; to the extent that we do not entertain doubts about eternal life, the devil cannot hold us with the fear of death, a fear which at one time could move us to any baseness; to the extent that we bear the cross of Christ, sufferings and persecution lead to the victory of good and not to its defeat.

The devil continues to reign only over those who remain

in evil. We are called to penetrate all the evil stratagems and world plans of evil and to destroy evil by the power of good, in patience and hope. Fear in the face of evil is more dangerous than evil. Evil is repulsive, but it gains strength when we are weak. Christianity gives mankind the opportunity to defeat evil at its very core—the rejection of God, universal enmity and deceit. God, love and truth all dwell already on earth in Christ.

Thus, Christianity does not promise deliverance from sufferings and death on the earth; in the world there is life and joy, but the world is stricken with evil and doomed to death. The path of the cross is essential for the Christian, but it is the path to life, and it is the path for the final triumph of life over evil. Evil is finally overcome through sufferings and death if they are in Christ for the Kingdom of God.

CONCLUSION

XXXIII

Christianity is the good news about the Kingdom of God, that is, about the union of all men and all things in God. We suffer because we ourselves and everything in the world are imperfect, distorted, doubleminded and unstable. In the Kingdom of God we find everything cleansed and transformed in Christ and in the Spirit: our own selves, other men and even the entire universe. We find in it the perfect image of goodness, truth and beauty. Of course, both we and the world are entering the Kingdom of God only gradually and partially; but we see within it the ideal image of all creation and we believe that it will someday be realized in all its fulness because all things have already been redeemed in Christ.

God dwells both within our souls and within the fallen world, but it is only in the Kingdom of God that we share a common life with Him. We unite ourselves with Him in all our spiritual perfections and in living a life in goodness, for He is the life, the unity and the source of all perfections. We unite ourselves with Him in that which is higher than all perfections: communion with the Father, Son and Holy Spirit. The highest gift of the Kingdom of God is communion with the life of the Holy Trinity. All of Christianity and all the universe is a revelation of the triune God: the revelation of the infinite value of that which is personal and unique in each being no matter how small and the equal value of the universal and perfect unity. It was said: "and God will be all in all." This means that everything will be filled with being, everything will be united in God. Even at this time we see all this.

People in this fallen world face both loneliness and union with others with equal fear. Loneliness is evil. But union with others also becomes evil when we unite ourselves in empty vanity or in evil. The greatest good for us is living in union with other people, but only when we are united by love and truth in communion with God and service to Him in all things. Christ the Lord and the Holy Spirit unite us through adoption to the one Father. This is precisely the unity in the all-perfect Spirit, in truth, love and every good thing, a unity in which we can embrace all men and all that exists. If three are united in the name of Christ, they will be strong and happy. If thousands are gathered in the Kingdom of God here on earth, the Christian world begins to be transformed. If millions desire to unite themselves in God, all humanity would be subject to the Church, for according to the words of Christ: blessed are the meek, for they shall inherit the earth.

Man can find happiness in unity with God and men, in closeness to all creation, in love, truth and beauty and in good works. All of this is realized on earth in the Church. In it the Kingdom of God dwells; it leads us to the Kingdom through faith and knowledge, sacraments and divine services and the life and activities of the Church society. He who remains in the Church on an external and earthly level only, internally betrays Christ; but no one should neglect even the simplest forms of Church life: every one of them can lead us to the Kingdom of God.

Christianity is not of this world, but it is directed toward

the world in order to lead it to God. The Christian cannot
renounce his duty with respect to people; but those who live
a peaceful life have a special calling to be Christians in that
life. Christianity cannot abandon the peaceful struggle for
the conquest of all humanity. Without Christianity humanity
will not find the true ideal of man and human society, will
not find the true God, true wisdom, goodness and beauty.
We bear a heavy responsibility for whatever transpires in the
world.

Christianity does not deceive us, promising immediate
deliverance from evil, sufferings and death: they will continue
to the end of history. But for the Christian the cross is the
strength and the path to joy. The New Testament gives testi-
mony to the fact that the victory of men and nations will be
crowned by the general transformation of the universe in
which God the Father, Christ and the Holy Spirit will dwell
with us in a visible way in blessedness, light and glory. Christians even now experience this in the Kingdom of God, though
it is as yet unseen by the world.

Catholicity and the Structures
of the Church

INTRODUCTION

The general meaning of the word "catholicity" in the understanding of linguists and theologians is approximately the following: catholicity means general, common, universal (in the qualitative and quantitative meaning), whole, total, existing and meaningful for all, at the same time one and plural, possessing organic unity.[1] In the Christian understanding, catholic means possessing the fulness of all positive qualities for all mankind;[2] accepted by the Church everywhere, always and by everyone;[3] possessing the wholeness of truth and holiness, infinitely multiform but united in God in faith and church organization. According to the Slavophiles, catholicity unites all Christians in faith, freedom and love, in the Holy Spirit, in the revelation of God and in Holy Tradition. Catholicity can be related to the whole universe inasmuch as it is renewed in Jesus Christ and inasmuch as the Church has the gift and purpose of communicating the fulness of God to the whole world.

Catholicity means in particular confessing true doctrine (Orthodoxy) or belonging to the Orthodox Church. In patristic thought, catholicity is not just an inner property of the Church—it is something manifested in her unity in time

[1]H.G. Liddell and R. Scott, *A Greek-English Lexicon,* 9th ed. (Oxford, 1940) 855; see also J.H. Maude, "Catholicism, Catholicity," in J. Hastings, ed., *Encyclopaedia of Religion and Ethics* (Edinburgh: T. & T. Clark, 1910) 3:258-61.
[2]St. Cyril of Jerusalem, *Catechetical Lectures* 18:23.
[3]St. Vincent of Lérins, *Commonitorium* 1:2.

and space, and also in the general organization of the Church (according to the Roman Catholics, in the papacy).[4] Finally, catholicity originates in the will of God the Father to save mankind. It is accomplished in Jesus Christ,[5] in Whom dwells saving fulness and perfection. Catholicity is given by the universal, lifecreating power of the Holy Spirit in a variety of His gifts.

The Protestant understanding differs from that of the Orthodox and Roman Catholics in that, for them, catholicity is seen as something limited and relative, or as comprehensiveness—a rather vague principle of unity acceptable to many. It can also be understood as something generally accepted by all mankind.[6]

The general, abstract idea of catholicity can be described thusly: any being in which unity and plurality are innerly united possesses catholicity. A being does not possess catholicity if it is comprised of parts united only externally. The unity on which catholicity can be based must possess a fulness of existence such that it would be capable of comprehending the whole being. This unity can possess two forms: it can be the principle from which all other forms of the being proceed (for example, Jesus Christ as the source of the existence of the Church); or, it can be a principle of consubstantiality, which determines from within the form of existence of all the component elements of the being (for example, the common nature of the Church of all nations throughout all ages).

The second principle of catholicity is plurality or variety, for consubstantiality does not exclude the variety of forms in which it can be realized (for example, in the Church, her members, church communities, local churches, etc.). However, each particular form of existence must: (1) participate in the unity and common nature of the whole; (2) be a positive element for all others and for the whole; and (3) include in itself all other forms of existence, or at least be with them in an inner communion. Thus, in the Church, everyone and everything is determined by God and Jesus

---

[4]G. Thils, "Catholicity," in the *New Catholic Encyclopedia,* 3:339-40.
[5]St. Ignatius of Antioch, *To the Smyrneans* 8.
[6]J. Salaverri, in *Lexikon für Theologie und Kirche* (1961) 6:90-1.

Christ and participates in the very nature of Christianity; everyone and everything has its positive meaning for all others and for the whole Church; everyone must be in total communion, each one with everyone. Such is the idea of the body of Christ in St. Paul: unity and multiformity are innerly united in the one body of the Church. This is what we call catholicity. If the Church were only one, plurality and variety would be excluded from her. But catholicity permits the unity of the Church to embrace all the various elements in her, in such a way as to enrich her without destroying her unity.

It is impossible in one article to exhaust all the sources of Orthodox theology. Therefore, we will limit ourselves to the general ideas of Orthodox dogmatics and to the teachings of the New Testament.

I

THE PROTOTYPE OF CATHOLICITY IN GOD

The prototype of the catholicity of the Church can undoubtedly be found in God Himself. God is one being, in Whom all is divine. The divine unity originates from God the Father. All exists from Him and for Him, not only in the world, but in God Himself—for the Son of God, the Holy Spirit and all the divine manifestations proceed from the Father and exist for the Father. The divine unity is eternally realized in the divine consubstantiality, in the unique divinity of the Holy Trinity from which proceed all the essential energies of God. Nevertheless, in the divine unity, each hypostasis is absolutely different from the others; each exists for the others and by the others; each includes in itself all others in eternal intercommunion. Each hypostasis manifests itself particularly within the unique action of God. The truth and wisdom of God, His life, holiness and love, all have their principle in God the Father. But the Son is the very hypostatical Wisdom, and the Holy Spirit is the Spirit of wisdom shining from the Son. The Holy Spirit is the very hypostatical

Life, holiness and love proceeding from the Father and dwelling in the Son. From God the Father, the divine wisdom and
lifecreating power are poured on the whole universe through
the Son of God and the Holy Spirit.

It is worthwhile to note that the Orthodox doctrine of
the self-revelation of God in ideas, energies and glory particularly stresses the correlation of unity and infinite plurality
in this divine self-revelation. The absolute simplicity of the
divine Superessence—the absolute unity of the Father, of the
Logos and of the Spirit—is manifested in the infinite plurality
of divine decisions, ideas, words and energies, and in the
infinite variety or forms of the divine glory. God is, as it were,
not satisfied by His superessential simplicity; He wants to
exist in the fulness of all possible forms of divine existence.
Nevertheless, the divine unity is never compromised—the
entire being of God is present in each of its manifestations,
and all the divine manifestations are united with each other
in the perfect harmony of the divine Being.

II

CATHOLICITY IN THE WORLD

The universe created by God reflects in itself the same
connection between unity and plurality in their ideal harmony.
The presence of God in the world unites it in God, but at
the same time God supports in existence not only the whole
cosmos but each creature, in the particularity of its own
existence. The divine words and energies are the foundations
of the existence of the innumerable created beings, uniting
them in common harmony.

In the fallen world, unity became confusion and variety
became division. The possibility of coherence and harmony
was lost. Either unity absorbs and excludes variety, suppress-
ing everything particular, or all is divided in reciprocal differences and hostile separations. Thus, catholicity scarcely exists
in this fallen world.

III

JESUS CHRIST AS THE SOURCE
OF CATHOLICITY

The harmony of unity in plurality, which was lost with the fall of mankind, has been restored in the world through the Church by the incarnation. The Son of God brings into the world the fulness of the divinity (John 1:16; Colossians 2:9), which fills all those in whom Christ dwells through faith and grace (Ephesians 3:19). "And the Word was made flesh, and dwelt among us, . . . full of grace and truth" (John 1:14).

In becoming man, the Son of God has brought down into the Church the divine truth itself and the manifold wisdom of God (Ephesians 3:10); He has revealed to man the image of God, the divine Logos, "in Whom are hid all the treasures of wisdom and knowledge" (Colossians 2:3).

The Son of God sent into the world the Holy Spirit, Who has rested in Him eternally, and thus the fulness of the gifts of the Spirit were poured onto the Church. The Son of God and the Holy Spirit not only revealed God to us, but brought us into communion with Him, adopting us to Him. In this way, man became both a participant in the divine nature (2 Peter 1:4) and a member of "the household of God," of the Father, of the Son and of the Holy Spirit (Ephesians 2:19-22). The perfection of God the Father was manifested to the faithful as the ideal of their life, and the love of the Father has embraced them and has lifted them to heaven through the Son and the Spirit.

Jesus Christ has united man with the superessential divine Being, in Whom the fulness of existence is not absorbed by unity. The Holy Trinity is the source of infinite illumination and lifegiving manifestations.

When the Son of God became man, He also restored the fulness of existence in human nature, which would have been impossible without the union of the human with the divine, i.e., without the divinization of man in Jesus Christ. As God and man, Jesus Christ unites in Himself the fulness of the perfection of existence of both God and man. That is why He can be called "Him that filleth all in all" (Ephesians 1:23).

Christ's fulness is not confined solely in Himself, just as the fulness of God the Father does not remain in Himself. The divinity of the Father is also the divinity of the Son and of the Holy Spirit, and Jesus Christ is consubstantial with all mankind.[7] Perhaps the most striking texts in this regard are in the parable of the last judgment (Matthew 25:31-46): Christ identifies Himself with man, but clearly in such a way that man does not cease to be a particular person. The unity of Christ with man is founded on the fact that He possesses the human nature common to all men, as well as on the fact of His free desire to be in others and to identify Himself freely with them. Those in whom Christ dwells—whether they are aware of His presence or not—cannot prevent Christ's presence in them. They can, however, either accept Christ in the measure of their faith and good will or reject Him. In any case, our transformation in Christ depends not only on the Lord, but also on us: Christ is in us, but we can be not in Him (2 Corinthians 3:6).

But even if we are in Christ, our existence is not confused by His. Each Christian realizes Christ in himself in his own way, although Christ is always identical to Himself (Hebrews 13:8). Christ is our prototype, first as the Logos, in Whom are contained the ideas of all creatures; second, as the Son of Man, Who, as the Son of God, existed from all eternity in the Father's divine contemplation. (We can think of the first Adam as being created according to the image of the Son of Man which existed eternally in God.) Thirdly, Christ is the image of the renewed man (1 Corinthians 15:42-49; Romans 8:29; Ephesians 2:10; Colossians 3:10). In this way, Jesus Christ became the New Adam (Romans 5; 1 Corinthians 15). Only he who is conformed to Christ can be a "new creature" (2 Corinthians 5:17; Galatians 6:15). Christ became for us our wisdom, righteousness, sanctification and redemption (1 Corinthians 1:30). In Him we have dignity,

[7]This is the dogma of the Fourth Ecumenical Council.

glory and the lifecreating heavenly Spirit (1 Corinthians 15:42-45).

From the fulness of Christ's humanity, all receive according to the measure of their faith and effort (Romans 12:3; Philippians 3:12-16). We are apprehended by Jesus Christ, but we can only strive to apprehend Him. Each Christian, even if he is relatively perfect, can be only a particular and partial image of Christ. He can become such an image not only because of all the gifts he received from Jesus Christ and the Holy Spirit, but also because of his own creative effort (Philippians 2:12-13, and others). We must "gather with Christ" (Luke 11:23). The Apostle Paul, who ascribed everything in his life to Jesus Christ and to the grace of the Holy Spirit, was nevertheless aware of the enormous effort of all his being which he made during his apostolic activity (1 Corinthians 1-3, 9; 2 Corinthians 4, 6, 10-13). Human efforts do not create any value—they only realize in their life and in the surrounding world what we receive from Christ and the Holy Spirit, although our efforts are always creative and personal. Without such human efforts, there would be no positive and creative variety in the Church, no living diversity, and therefore no catholicity.

IV

CATHOLICITY AND THE CHURCH AS THE BODY OF CHRIST

"He that is joined unto the Lord is one spirit [with the Lord]" (1 Corinthians 6:17). Our bodies are also members of Christ, for "by one Spirit are we all baptized into one body . . . and have been all made to drink into one Spirit" (1 Corinthians 6:15, 12:13). We are all one body, one Christ (1 Corinthians 12:20-27; Romans 12:5; cf Ephesians 5:22-23). The fulness of Christ is communicated to the Church and comprehends her: the Church is the "fulness of Him that

filleth all in all" (Ephesians 1:23). The Church is the Kingdom of the beloved Son of the Father, of the Son of God
from Whom all is derived and in Whom all is supported
(Colossians 1:13, 14-23). The fulness, which according to
the will of God the Father must dwell in His Son, is, we can
think, divinity itself, and the universe and the Church in
particular—they were created by God and they are in God
through His Son and the Holy Spirit. We are "complete" in
Christ (Colossians 2:10), i.e., we have received in ourselves
His fulness. The Lord has loved the Church and has sacrificed
Himself for her to communicate to her the fulness of perfection (Ephesians 5:25-27) and the riches of glory and to make
every man perfect (Colossians 1:27-28). Christ descended to
earth and "to the lower parts of the earth," and He ascended
into heaven, "that He might fill all things" (Ephesians 4:9-
10).

Christians, as members of Christ's body, proceed from
Christ—we are "of His flesh, and of His bones" (Ephesians
5:30). We are all branches growing on the vine which is
Christ (John 15:1-8). The book of Revelation also speaks
about those who are from the seed of the Church, that is,
those who are born of the Church (Revelation 12:17; cf
Galatians 4:26-28). The idea of the motherhood of the
Church has become commonplace in Holy Tradition, although,
strictly speaking, Christians are born of God in Jesus Christ
by the grace of the Holy Spirit (John 1:12-13). Nevertheless,
we are not born without an action of the Church and, in the
Church, being associated with her nature. The Apostles Peter
and Paul particularly underline the generation of Christians
from the Word of God, which was preached in words and
by the very life of the apostles (1 Peter 1:23; Romans 10:14-
17; 1 Corinthians 4:14-16; Galatians 4:19). The same word
of God is preached continuously by the Church. It would not
be false to say that the Church gives birth to her new members, but according to the will of God, by the power of the
Holy Spirit, and only in Christ. The Lord Jesus Christ is
evidently not born from the Church—He is the head of the
Church from Whom is the whole body (Colossians 2:19).
God the Father "hath put all things under His feet, and gave

Him to be the head over all things to the church" (Ephesians 1:22).[8]

Christ is not dependent on the Church or on her members, but the whole Church and each individual Christian are in absolute dependence, although freely, upon Christ. The symbol of marriage between Christ and the Church shows us that the Church can be distinguished from Christ as some kind of "collective person" in the same way as each Christian can be totally identified with Christ, being a particular person. At the same time, if a husband who loves his wife loves himself, Christ also loves Himself in the Church, that is, in His body,[9] because Christ and the Church are hypostatically different, but they are one being. The initiative of the marriage with the Church, according to Ephesians 5, belongs to Christ, and Christ Himself makes this marriage possible by His love and self-denial, purifying the Church from every spot and blemish and making her perfect in everything. It would be false, however, to conclude from this text that the Church is passive in her relationship with Christ.

The unity and plurality of the Church is manifested also in her eucharistic life. "We being many are one bread, and one body: for we are all partakers of that one bread," writes St. Paul (1 Corinthians 10:17; cf John 6:56). Jesus Christ distributes His body to all Christians, and His blood, which is shed for us, He gives us to drink. He, as it were, sacrificially

[8]The book of Revelation (12:1-5) states that "the woman clothed with the sun" on the one hand "was with child and cried travailing in birth." On the other hand, her child was appointed "to rule all nations with a rod of iron and was caught up unto God and to His throne." According to Methodius of Olympus and Andrew of Crete, the first verse speaks of Christ, inasmuch as He is identified with the persecuted Christians (cf the words of Christ to the Apostle Paul when he saw the Lord on the way to Damascus). The second verse perhaps speaks about the Mother of God, who possibly is representing the Old Testament Church. See E.B. Allo, *La clé de l'Apocalypse* (Paris, 1938) 178.

[9]Ephesians 5:28-29. In Revelation 22:17, the Church, as a particular person, refers to Christ together with the Holy Spirit. Strictly speaking, however, a person can never be collective, because the person is necessarily unique and different from all other persons. The idea of a "collective" person can be reduced to the idea of a collectivity considered as being particular and different from all similar collectivities—e.g., this family, as opposed to all other families; this nation, in contrast to all other nations; or this local church in her particularity, as distinct from all other churches.

divides Himself among us, giving Himself to each of us in order to dwell in all. But the eucharistic presence of Christ saves only those who partake worthily—first of all those who examine themselves and change themselves. Without a personal effort to prepare ourselves for the reception of Christ, eucharistic communion can even be dangerous for our lives (1 Corinthians 11:27-32).

The growth of the Church and of those in the Church is described by St. Paul in two different perspectives. On the one hand, the whole body is from Christ (Ephesians 4:16; Colossians 2:19), without whom we can achieve nothing (John 15:5). All is from Christ and is accomplished by Him in His divine and human sacrificial life (Colossians 1:12-23). On the other hand, we can build up the body of Christ, we can grow in the unity of the faith and in the knowledge of the Son of God, we can strive toward His fulness and grow in the truth and love of Christ. Each part (*meros* in Greek) of the Church acts in this case in its own measure but in unity with others (Ephesians 4:12-16; Colossians 2:19). If we are "grounded" and "settled" in the faith, we receive all the gifts of the Kingdom, of eternal life, of universal reconciliation and holiness from the fulness of Christ (Colossians 1:12-23). Men can add nothing to the divine and human fulness of Christ, but each Christian and entire Christian communities creatively realize what is given to them in Christ in their own measure and particular form.

It is necessary that the body be comprised of many members: "For the body is not one member, but many. . . . And if they were all one member, where were the body?" (1 Corinthians 12:14, 19; cf Romans 12:4-5). This assertion of the Apostle Paul is of very great importance: a separated person or individual is not a complete being. We can apply this even to Christ: the purpose of His advent was to not remain in His divine perfection, but to unite in Himself man with God; and also to not remain a unique, divinized, perfect man, but to unite in Himself all mankind and the whole universe in order to transform all creatures and to give everyone the possibility of freely acquiring a perfect existence. Our Lord Jesus Christ contained the Church in Himself even before her foundation, just as He was the Son of Man and the Lamb of God even before His incarnation. Nevertheless, only the incarnation made Him truly man, and only with its full realization by the Church through the submission of all creatures to Christ will that which was before the ages and already at the time of the ascension of the Son of God be totally accomplished. Only then will the fulness of existence of the whole universe and every creature be achieved and will God be all in all.

A particular being's existence is not perfect outside of the whole reality, but the existence of anything particular is absolutely necessary for the whole and is in itself positive. Each member of the body, each vocation and gift is necessary (1 Corinthians 12:21-22, 28-30; Romans 12:3-8). This is the foundation of the existence of the Church and her organization. Without the diversity of the members neither the Church nor the world could exist, just as God Himself would not be perfect if He would not be the Holy Trinity—although the essence of God is one and the Church possesses one and the same nature, and although the whole universe in fact is united by general principles.

The particular is compatible with the whole. Even more than this, all the members are not only members of the body but of each other (Romans 12:5). If each member is necessary for each and every other member, the more is it necessary for the whole body. The difference between the members does not prevent them from belonging to the same body. "If the foot shall say, Because I am not the hand, I am not of the body; is it therefore not of the body?" (1 Corinthians 12:15) "If the whole body were an eye, where were the hearing? . . . But now God hath set the members every one of them in the body, as it hath pleased Him" (1 Corinthians 12:17-18). Each member is necessary to all and to the whole body, and no member is self-sufficient: "the eye cannot say unto the hand, I have no need of thee . . . Nay, much more those members of the body, which seem to be more feeble, are necessary" (1 Corinthians 12:21-22).

The Holy Trinity produces variety in the Church and distributes the divine gifts, although all are derived from the

divine unity and return to it. "Now there are diversities of
gifts, but the same Spirit. And there are differences of admin-
istrations, but the same Lord. And there are diversities of
operations, but it is the same God which worketh all in all.
But the manifestation of the Spirit is given to every man to
profit withal. . . . all these worketh that one and the selfsame
Spirit, dividing to every man severally as He will" (1 Corinthians 12:4-7, 11).[10]

On the very day of Pentecost, there "appeared unto them
cloven tongues like as of fire, and it sat upon each of them"
(Acts 2:3). It is remarkable how, at the very moment of the
foundation of the Church, the Holy Spirit transformed not
masses of men but each man individually, although uniting
them at once in perfect unity. The gift of tongues enabled
the apostles to unite to the Church people of different nations.
St. John Chrysostom adds that the apostles became torches
from which many other torches were kindled.[11] The fulness
of the Holy Spirit was poured out on the whole world,
sanctifying and unifying all those who are obedient to God
with the Church (Acts 5:32). We see here again all the
elements of catholicity.

The members or "parts" of the Church are in need of each
other; but they must also be united by the common love, by
the love of peace, the help of each other, unanimity and
compassion—that is, by a positive communion (Romans 12:9-
18; 1 Corinthians 12:25-13:13; Colossians 3:15).

---

[10]The word "Spirit" in verse 4 certainly refers to the Holy Spirit; the
word "Lord" in verse 5 refers to the Son of God; and the word "God" in
verse 6 means God the Father. This is the opinion of St. John Chrysostom,
Homilies on 1 Corinthians 29:23.

[11]*Homilies on Acts* 4:2.

V

ST. JOHN CHRYSOSTOM'S TEACHING ABOUT THE BODY OF CHRIST

St. John Chrysostom has a very remarkable and deep understanding of St. Paul's idea of the body of Christ.[12] The body is the image of the whole being, especially inasmuch as this being depends on its head. The head of the Church is Jesus Christ: from Him she has her life and dwelling, in Him she is growing in God. To separate from the Church means to lose life. Inasmuch as the Church is the body of its head (Christ), she can be identified with Christ. Generally speaking, the body of Christ can be determined as the unity "of the faithful of the whole world who live now, who lived in the past and of those who will live in the future." The body is inseparable from the Spirit. The body of Christ is formed by the Holy Spirit: we are baptized by Him into "one body."

The body of Christ is one and the same. Inasmuch as the members of the Church belong to the one body, they are all identical. Unity and plurality, as it were, coincide in the Church. The plurality in the Church is no less real than the unity. The members of the Church are really different. "If we would not be really different, we could not be one body, and not being one body, we could not be one." God communicates to us different gifts, corresponding to the particular character of each one of us.

For St. John Chrysostom, the members of the body of Christ are not only Christians individually but also make up entire categories of Christians (for example: different ranks of hierarchs and ministers; benefactors; the poor; virgins; women, etc.) and also local churches, which he opposes to the "Church all over the world," saying that "the body of the Church is formed by many churches."

All members of the Church are necessary; all have their

[12]*Homilies on Romans* 21 (on 12:4-6); *Homilies on 1 Corinthians* 30-33 (on 12:12-30); *Homilies on Ephesians* 10 (on 4:4-16); *Homilies on Colossians* 7 (on 2:19).

own purpose of existence. In this respect they are all equal, although they can have different degrees of importance. Any wrong from which one member will suffer will wrong the whole Church. When the Church is deprived of one of her members, she is, as it were, "divided." The well-being of each member of the Church cannot be separated from the well-being of all her other members and of the Church as a whole. Therefore, each member of the Church must firmly keep his own position in the totality of the life of the Church. The members of Christ are members of each other.

No member of the Church is self-sufficient; likewise, without the unity of her members the Church cannot be the Church. The supposition that one member of the Church can be the whole body of Christ is unnatural. No member of the Church can replace another; that is why there must be many. Each member is necessary for the perfection and beauty of any other member and of the whole Church.

God wants man to cooperate with Him. The life of the members of the Church and consequently of the whole Church is not possible without freedom and free human, creative effort.

If the body of Christ is "unity in variety," it cannot exist without the communion of all the members, without common love, reciprocal care and common interdependence. Common sympathy and common care for the common good harmoniously unite the Church in one body.

This teaching of St. John Chrysostom is a most excellent example of the doctrine of catholicity. It is quite remarkable that the holy father finds the principle of catholicity, as he himself said, "in absolutely everything," particularly in the elements of nature, in plants, in our bodies, in art and in culture.

VI

OTHER SYMBOLS OF CATHOLICITY

The allegorical description of the Church as a temple contains the same theology as that of the body of Christ. Christ is the cornerstone; on Him the whole structure is built. But the apostles and prophets also belong to the foundation of the Church, and all Christians "as lively stones, are built up a spiritual house" in faith and obedience (1 Peter 2:3-10; Ephesians 2:19-20), and "all the building fitly framed together groweth unto a holy temple in the Lord: in whom ye also are builded together for a habitation of God through the Spirit" (Ephesians 2:21-22). Thus, God has included the prophets and apostles in the very foundation of the Church, and all Christians are harmoniously united by their life and faith in one Church. In the future world, God Himself will be the Temple in which man will live (Revelation 21-22).

A similar meaning is reflected in the parable of one shepherd with one flock of sheep who know the voice of their pastor and follow everywhere after him (John 10:1-16). The idea of an active following after Christ, which includes the necessity of sharing His cross, is mentioned very often by our Lord (Matthew 8:22, 10:38, 16:24, 19:21, and others).

Jesus Christ has united Himself with all that is human. He even took upon Himself our sins, our sufferings and death. We also must unite ourselves with Him in His sufferings and death, in His obedience, holiness and wisdom, in order to participate in His eternal life and resurrection, in His Kingdom and divinity (2 Corinthians 5; Romans 5, 6, 8; Philippians 2:1-5). Wherever even two or three are united in the name of Christ, He will be with them (Matthew 18:20).

If we are in Christ we are one, because He cannot be divided (1 Corinthians 1:12-15). Variety is not division. The catholicity of the Church implies not only the churches on earth but also the heavenly Church, with which we are in communion.[13] This unity is built on the unity of the Kingdom of God, in which all members of the Church both on earth and in heaven participate. The unity of the earthly and the heavenly Church is probably one of the best expressions of catholicity, inasmuch as this union includes such extremely

[13]Ephesians 1:10, 2:5-6; Colossians 1:20, 3:1-4; Philippians 3:20; Hebrews 12:22-24; Revelation 1:19-20, 4, 6:9-11, 7:9-17, 14, 15, 19:1-18.

different forms of Christian life as the life of the Kingdom of
Heaven and life on earth.

VII

CATHOLICITY AND TRUTH

The unity and all-comprehensiveness of truth has a particular meaning for the catholicity of the Church. Jesus Christ
emphasizes the unity of truth in God. He very often stresses
that the truth is, as it were, primarily in the Father and
proceeds from Him. The Son of God has the truth from the
Father, and the same truth is announced by the Holy Spirit
(John 8:26-28, 40; 12:49-50; 16:12-15; 17:17). The apostles
are established in the same truth, which they have learned in
God through Christ and the Holy Spirit (Galatians 1:6-12).
Because of this, the Church becomes the "pillar" and "ground"
of the unique truth (1 Timothy 3:15), which remains eternally unchangeable, as does Christ Himself (Hebrews 13:8;
2 Timothy 2:11-13; 2 Corinthians 1:19-22). "Heaven and
earth shall pass away, but My words shall not pass away"
(Matthew 24:35). This is also the reason for the unity of
Holy Tradition: if the divine truth is one, like God Himself,
how can Holy Tradition change? We must have the same
mind as Christ (Philippians 2:5); we must be established in
our holy faith and "earnestly contend for the faith which
was once delivered unto the saints" (Jude 3; cf 1 Peter 3:8;
Romans 12:16). We have one Lord, one Father, one God and
the Father of all (Ephesians 4:5-6; Galatians 3:25-29). Following the example of the community of Jerusalem, the whole
Church has firmly remained in the teaching of the apostles
(Acts 2:42).

The truth, however, does not remain, so to speak, "im-
movable." Even in God it has different forms: it is identical
to the essence of the Father, it is His hypostatical Logos and
Wisdom, and it is also the Spirit of truth and wisdom. The

truth of the Father through the hypostatical Truth which is the Son shines in the Holy Spirit. The light of the divine truth and "the manifold wisdom of God" (Ephesians 3:10) fill the Church and the whole cosmos. God manifests Himself and speaks to man "at sundry times and in divers manners" (Hebrews 1:1-2). The incarnation brought the divine truth to earth. The apostles and the whole Church preach it throughout the world (Matthew 28:19-20; Mark 16:15-20; Romans 10:14-21; Colossians 1:3-9). Man is regenerated by the word of God (1 Peter 1:23), and this divine word is the seed of the Kingdom of God in man's soul (Matthew 13). The truth is freely accepted or rejected by man.[14] The possibility of knowledge in general and the knowledge of God is given to all men (John 1:9; Romans 1:18-20). But inasmuch as sin and fleshliness has blinded man (Romans 1:21-32; 2 Corinthians 3:6-15, 4:4), God, through Christ and the Holy Spirit, restores in us the capability of understanding and transforms (regenerates) our minds (2 Corinthians 3-4; 1 John 2, 5:20; 1 Corinthians 2; Romans 12:2; Ephesians 4:23).

Knowledge of truth must grow throughout the world and in every Christian (Matthew 13; Colossians 1:1-10). But can we admit variety in truth or in our knowledge and understanding of it? We cannot doubt that truth exists in many forms, because God is the Trinity and He reveals Himself in infinite forms of His Logos and Wisdom. This variety exists in eternal and perfect unity. In a certain sense we can speak about the unity and catholicity of the truth in itself and in its revelation. Each divine truth (logos or idea) is necessary as such, and is necessary also for all other truths and for the whole truth in its wholeness. All truths are reciprocally necessary and are determined by each other. All of them reveal the unique truth and, as it were, derive from its fulness.

The diversity of truth in human knowledge and understanding is also undeniable. It is evident already in the differences of degrees and fulness of our knowledge. It is enough to remember the teaching of St. Paul about "milk and hard food" in his apostolic teaching (1 Corinthians 3:1-4; Hebrews

[14]John 3:20-21, 5:24, 8:31-49, 9:39-41, 10:1-14, 12:37-41, 16:27-29; Matthew 13; 2 John 1-2.

5:11-6:6). From this fact alone follows the inevitability of the infinite diversity of knowledge of truth among the members of the Church. Omniscience is not possible for any man, and cannot even be ascribed to the Church in its human membership. It is proper only to God.

All that exists is manifested as truth (cf Ephesians 5:13) and has its logos or idea. Thus, the number of subjects of knowledge is practically inexhaustible, not only in general but even in theology. In each subject of knowledge there are many aspects, and there are many possible perspectives in which to study them. Therefore, each member of the Church and even the local churches are inevitably limited in their actual knowledge at every moment of their existence. Nevertheless, the possibility of the infinite deepening and widening of our knowledge and therefore the possibility of finding an answer to any possible question is given to the Church always and everywhere, inasmuch as even partial knowledge is partial knowledge of the unique, absolute truth contained in Christ and the Holy Spirit and manifested to those in the Church. As a consequence of the indivisibility of the truth, the knowledge of each truth opens to us the way to the knowledge of all other truths and the deepening of the knowledge of the truth in its totality.

Scholars do not pay sufficient attention to the personal form of the existence of truth, which is, of course, identical to itself in its essence. In divine revelation we find the doctrine of God the Father as the "only wise God" (Jude 25; Romans 16:27; 1 Timothy 1:17), of the Son of God as the hypostatical Wisdom and Logos, and of the Holy Spirit as the Spirit of wisdom and truth (Isaiah 11:2; John 15:26). All this bears witness that the one and the same divine truth and wisdom has three different personal forms. The teachings of St. John and St. Paul do not contradict each other, but it is impossible not to notice the very deep personal spirit and form in all their writings. In the same way, in the whole Church also each truth, although essentially one, is perceived by each Christian in a personal manner. Because of the personal perception of truth in God and in man, the truth is not only a subject of knowledge and of abstract thinking, but a real and living power by which any person lives (and there is no such thing as an impersonal life).

If the truth, being one in itself, is known in manifold forms and in a different measure by each individual Christian and by individual Christian communities, the knowledge of each Christian and of each local church has to complete the knowledge of others and depend on them. The fulness of knowledge is thus given to the Church in its catholicity, through the common witness of all the witnesses of truth: the prophets, the apostles, the fathers, the councils and all the saints. To put it another way, we can say, together with St. Vincent of Lérins and the Slavophiles, that perfect knowledge of truth is given to the Church only in her catholic unity.

In the light of the doctrine of the catholic character of truth and its knowledge in the Church, we can see how the catholicity of knowledge became a synonym for Orthodoxy. Orthodoxy, indeed, is nothing other than the affirmation and glorification of one truth, revealed to the Church and understood by her from the day of Pentecost. The Church exists only where the one truth is confessed—that is, where Orthodoxy is. Orthodoxy is not a collection of contradictory opinions, but the fulness of knowledge of the catholic Church.

Diversity has nothing to do with contradiction, which, from the time of the apostles, has always been considered by the Church as heresy. It is worthwhile to note that contemporary heretical theology tries, on the one hand, to find in Holy Scripture and Holy Tradition as many contradictions as possible, in order to undermine their authority. On the other hand, this theology, being inspired by relativism, denies the very existence of contradiction and heresies, insisting that there are only differences of opinions, which must be explained by the influence of different spiritual surroundings in different epochs. The oneness of truth is denied.

If we extract isolated texts and ideas from Holy Scripture and Holy Tradition, it is easy to find seeming contradictions in them. Genuine theology, in its understanding of revelation, always applied the principle of (if we may say so) "gnosiological catholicity." The entire content of scripture and tradition, expressed in so many books, texts and ideas, must be considered as one whole, each element of which depends on all others and on their totality. The only correct understanding is the one that unites the particular with the whole and understands everything in the light of the truth and in the totality of its content. In scripture and tradition, everything is complementary, and each element explains every other. All is necessary for the understanding of the whole. The foundation of theology is the knowledge of God, and theology must be built in the perspective of this knowledge.

There is only one teacher and one true doctrine for the Church: Jesus Christ and His teaching (Matthew 23:8). "Whosoever transgresseth, and abideth not in the doctrine of Christ, hath not God" (2 John 9). The preservation of the purity—that is, Orthodoxy—of Christ's teaching is of exceptional importance (Galatians 1:6-12; 2 Corinthians 4:1-6). All teachers who do not follow Christ or who deform His teaching are useless even for themselves, like spoiled food (Hebrews 13:7-9). All fleshly, worldly and purely human doctrines and all myths can be harmful (Colossians 2:4-23; Philippians 3:17-21; 2 Timothy 4:2-5). St. Paul violently rejects the pharisaical Judaism (Galatians 1:6-12; Philippians 3:1-11). Our Lord Jesus Christ proclaims that all that is purely human (inasmuch as it is consciously or unconsciously opposed to God) and pharisaical Judaism (which is opposed to Him) is derived from Satan (Matthew 16:22-23; John 8:40-49).

VIII

CATHOLICITY AND ETHICS

God is holy because His existence and life are perfect. If the Son of God and the Holy Spirit have life from the Father (John 5:26, 15:26), Their holiness is also from the Father. Is the Son of God not the truth and the Logos of holiness, and is the Holy Spirit not the very holy, hypostatical Life?[15] Thus, the divine holiness, as the divine truth, is manifested in three hypostatical forms. Human holiness, in its perfection, is realized and manifested only in Jesus Christ. The Church is called to accomplish the holiness of Christ in her whole existence and in all her members. The source and nature of holiness are one, but its forms among Christians are infinitely diverse, and impersonal holiness is impossible. It is enough to point to the multitude of ranks of holiness recognized by our Church. Here again the principle of catholicity is evidently at work: different personal forms and general types of holiness complete each other, all being necessary for the life of the Church. In the same way, moral perfection recognizes a correlation of all virtues and cannot be reduced to only one of them, even if it will be love, for genuine love in itself unites all virtues.

Outside of love there is no catholicity. Love strives to give existence to others and to live in communion with them. Love produces and unites all beings. The source of love is in God the Father and in the Son and Spirit of His love (Romans 5:5; Colossians 1:13; 1 John 4:16). The divine love of the Holy Trinity is poured out onto the Church through Jesus Christ and the grace of the Holy Spirit. Love is the cause of the incarnation and redemption (John 3:16; 1 John 4:7-5:3; Romans 5:8). Love is the cause of the apostolic mission and of any growth of the Church (Ephesians 4:16). We find in the New Testament a doctrine about divine love and the love of Christ which dwell and act in Christians depending on their faith and dedication to God.[16] Divine love and Christian love, which flows from it, build up and unite the Church. In both cases, love as a power of spiritual life and of activity has as many different forms and immediate objects as there

[15]The idea that the holiness of the Father is manifested in the Holy Spirit is found in the theology of St. Cyril of Alexandria. Hubert Du Manoir de Juaye, *Dogme et spiritualité chez saint Cyrille d'Alexandrie* (Paris, 1944) 246-9.

[16]Luke 11:42; John 15:9-10; 1 John 2:5-10, 2:15, 3:10, 3:17, 4:7-5:3; Jude 21; Romans 8:39; 1 Corinthians 8:1-3; 2 Thessalonians 3:5; 2 Corinthians 5:14-15; Philippians 1:8; Ephesians 4:19.

are Christians and churches. Love flows out from God, within the whole Church and throughout the world. The responding love of Christians animates the whole body of the Church and converges on God. Without the divine love and Christ's love there would be no love at all, and each manifestation of true love is precious to God and for the Church, for it expresses the goodness of mankind.

IX

CATHOLICITY AND UNIVERSALITY

Catholicity in itself necessarily includes universality. First, the very nature of God, of Christ and of the Church, in its fulness, is, so to speak, "open" and can be communicated to many persons and beings. All creatures can participate in God through Jesus Christ and the grace of the Holy Spirit. All mankind can participate in the Church. Only those who consciously and freely are opposed to God and to the Church can never be in union with them. Secondly, the purpose of the existence of God and of man alike does not imply self-limitation, but, on the contrary, a maximum expansion of their existence. This is the evident reason for the creation and the incarnation. The whole universe must become the Kingdom of God. All of creation must be "drawn into the nets" of the Kingdom (Matthew 13:47-50; 1 Corinthians 15:20-28; Revelation 21-22). All of mankind, all nations and even all "the poor, and the maimed, and the halt, and the blind" are called into the Kingdom (Matthew 28:19; Luke 13:29, 14: 21-23). The Holy Spirit descended in order to transform the whole cosmos. All beings are valuable not only, so to speak, in their nature, which they have received from the general treasury of existence, but also in their personal and particular realizations.

The whole universe is given to the Son of God by His Father (Luke 10:22; John 17:2). Our Lord has redeemed, reconciled and united all (John 10:1-16; Ephesians 1-2; Colossians 1). The very death of Christ on the cross attracts everyone to Him (John 12:32). In His personal preaching ministry, Jesus Christ "went about all the cities and villages, teaching in their synagogues, and preaching the gospel of the Kingdom" (Matthew 9:35-38), and He even went beyond the limits of Israel (Mark 7:24-31).

God, through Jesus Christ and the Holy Spirit, transmitted all the treasures of perfection and salvation to the apostles.[17] The apostles kept it in the unity of their college and in the apostolic community (Acts 2:42, 5:32; Galatians 1:18-2:10; see also the texts in the previous footnote). From the apostolic Church, Christianity spread by Holy Tradition throughout the world, in order to accomplish its universality (1 Corinthians 11:2; Ephesians 3; Colossians 1:23-29; Philippians 3; 2 Timothy 3:10-17).

X

THE CHURCH AND THE CHURCHES

The word "church" is used in the New Testament both in the singular[18] and in the plural,[19] and also in relation to the particular local churches.[20] Sometimes the texts speak about the Church in general, although dwelling in different localities.[21] St. Paul also uses an expression which in English is

[17]Acts 5:32; 1 Corinthians 7:25, 11:1-2; 2 Corinthians 3:1-6, 4:1-6, 13:3; Galatians 1:6-12, 16; Ephesians 2:20, 3:5-13.

[18]For example, Matthew 16:18, 18:17; Acts 2:47, 20:28; 1 Corinthians 10:32, 12:28; Ephesians 1:22, 3:10, 5:23; Colossians 1:18, 24; 1 Timothy 3:15.

[19]For example, Acts 14:23-28, 15:41, 16:5; 1 Peter 1:1-2; Romans 16:4, 16; 1 Corinthians 4:17, 16:1; 2 Corinthians 8, 9:8, 9:28, 12:13; Galatians 1:22; Philippians 4:15; 2 Thessalonians 1:4.

[20]For example, Acts 14:27; 3 John 9; Romans 16:1, Colossians 4:16; 1 Timothy 5:16; Revelation 3, 4.

[21]For example, Acts 20:17, 20; James 5:14; Romans 16:23; 1 Corinthians 1:2; Ephesians 1:1; Colossians 1:2; 1 Timothy 3:5.

translated "the church that is in the house"—in other words, a family with the whole household is considered a small church community.[22]

Such use of the word "church" in the New Testament can easily be explained in terms of catholicity. Essentially, the Church is one because her nature is one and because she unites all Christians in one God and in one Christ. Inasmuch as the Church is always identical to herself wherever she is, we can speak about the Church being present in any place where we find a Christian community. For the same reason, all church communities or local churches can rightly be called churches, and the same can be said about any genuine Christian family.

The description of the churches in the book of Acts, in the apostolic epistles and in the book of Revelation witnesses that they were different in their spiritual character and in their importance within the Church. With the development of the local churches, their particular characteristics were developed. We see the same phenomenon in the growth of monasticism, in its different forms, and in the development of the theological schools, in their variety (for example, Alexandrian, Antiochian, etc.). Variety always enriched the Church, as long as continuous communion between the churches and between all the different spiritual and theological trends—that is, the spirit of catholicity—was maintained by the churches.

The one Church comprehends (embraces) all churches, wherever and whenever they existed, on earth or in heaven. Therefore, the Church will certainly include the whole universe (Revelation 21-22). According to the doctrine of the body of Christ, any harm or any loss to any member or part of the Church hurts the whole Church. The perfection of the Church lies not only in her divine and human nature but also in her comprehensive character, in the infinite diversity of her members—consequently, in her catholicity. In the Kingdom of Heaven and in the future world, each individual will receive his reward, his particular form and degree of perfection (1

[22]For example, 1 Corinthians 16:19; Romans 16:4; Colossians 4:15; Philemon 1:2; 1 Timothy 3:5.

Corinthians 15:37-41). The nations will bring their particular glory (Revelation 21:26), and God, together with Jesus Christ, will prepare mansions for everyone (John 14:1-3). Jews and Greeks, men and women, persons of all social classes and positions, all become one and the same in Jesus Christ. They do not wish to remain simply Jews, Greeks, men, women, etc.—on the contrary, all natural and personal qualities are transformed and perfected in God. "As God hath distributed to every man, as the Lord hath called every one, so let him walk. And so ordain I in all churches. . . . let every man, wherein he is called, therein abide with God" (1 Corinthians 7:17, 24). St. Paul himself became everything for everyone, because he saw in this the best way to bring all to salvation (1 Corinthians 9:19-23).

XI

CATHOLICITY AND DIVISIONS

Catholicity presupposes diversity, but not contradictions or divisions, which are always condemned by the New Testament. One of the main causes of divisions is falsehood in all its forms: heresies, distortions of Christian doctrines, stupidity, love of myths, etc.[23] Other causes of divisions are love of this world, fleshliness and passions. The spirit of "this world" pushes man to divisions. The desire for possession of material goods often brings open struggle.[24] St. Paul pays special attention to the tendency of false Judaism to ruin Christian unity (Philippians 3:1-11; Galatians 1-6). The primary cause of divisions is always Satan (Luke 22:31; 2 Corinthians 11:13-14). If diversity enriches the Church, divisions destroy her.

The Church not only condemns divisions, but she excom-

[23]2 John 9-11; Galatians 1:6-12; Romans 16:17-18; Titus 3:9-11; Hebrews 13:9.
[24]Acts 6:1-6; Jude 17-21; 1 Corinthians 1:12-15, 3; Galatians 5:12-26; Colossians 2:4-23; Philippians 3:17-21; 2 Timothy 4:2-5.

municates from her catholicity all those who deny the very
nature of her existence. Evil cannot and must not belong to
the Church.[25] Behind every evil stands Satan—the source of
hatred, falsehood and death (John 8:37-49). "What concord
hath Christ with Belial? or what part hath he that believeth
with an infidel?" (2 Corinthians 6:15; cf 1 Corinthians 10:16-
22) Those who reject Christ cannot be members of the
Church.[26] Those who deny Christ and His Spirit belong neither
to Christ nor to the Church. They can be members of the
Church only in appearance (1 John 2:19; Romans 8:9). Those
who are not obedient to the Church are also excommunicated
from her (Matthew 18:15-18). This world is not compatible
with Christ or with the Church (John 14:21-24; 15:18-25;
16:33; 17:9, 14-16). The new man—that is, man regenerated
in Christ, the true Christian—and the old or corrupted man
of this world likewise are not compatible (Ephesians 2, 5;
Colossians 2-3). This world is evil, corruption and death
(Luke 9:57-62).

Renunciation of the world is an absolute condition for
genuine participation in the Church (Luke 14:31-35; Acts
2:40; Romans 6:1-11). Those who refuse to take upon themselves the cross of Christ cannot be His disciples (Luke 14:
27). Even those who are weak in goodness (those who have
lost their salt), or the lukewarm who try to keep neutral
between good and evil and who are sure in their earthly
prosperity, must be cast out of the Kingdom (Luke 14:34-35;
Revelation 3:15-18).

Does the New Testament recognize the existence of at
least partial good outside the Church? Certainly yes, although
this partial goodness in the world does not justify the identification of the Church with the world. Nevertheless, the
Church, discovering goodness outside of her limits, can be
in communication with the positive forces of the world (e.g.,
with the state), and Christians can participate in the life of
this world, inasmuch as it does not involve them in evil. For

[25]Matthew 13:24-30, 13:37-43, 21:33-46; Luke 13:23-28; 1 Corinthians
5:7-13; Titus 2:13-14.
[26]Matthew 10:32-41; Luke 11:23, 12:51-53, 14:24-27; John 15:5-6; Hebrews 6:4-8; Philippians 3:7-11.

the Church, the criterion for appreciation of good and evil is always the same—the divine truth revealed to her.

The possibility of certain positive relations between the Church and the heterodox denominations is built on the same principle. In spite of all the defects and deviations of heterodoxy, we can recognize that other denominations preserved some elements from the Church even after separating themselves from her. Thus, there is certain limited, common ground for faith and life between the Orthodox Church and the heterodox denominations.

XII

FALSE THEORIES OF CATHOLICITY

In conclusion, I would like to say a few words about theories of catholicity that seem to me to be false.

Some theologians exclude from catholicity the principle of universality. Others reduce catholicity only to the external spreading of Christianity. The first disregard the value and necessity for the Church of embracing or at least approaching all men, societies and nations. They ignore the fact that the members of the Church are valuable in and of themselves and enrich the Church by their diversity. The origin and the nature of the Church is one, but it is positively realized in its infinite diversity. The members of the Church must not be like coins of the same value. The universality of the Church is the will of God.

If universality is understood superficially, as the external unity of men and church organizations without their inner, essential unity, such an understanding of catholicity is certainly false.

Modern eucharistic ecclesiology reduces catholicity to the fact of the celebration of the Holy Liturgy in all church communities: the Church is where the liturgy is served, and all other principles of the life of the Church are considered unessential. It is absolutely false and even impossible to reduce the whole life of the Church to only one sacrament, or to separate the eucharist itself from all other fundamental forms of Christianity (for example, the knowledge of truth, the spiritual and moral life, etc.).

The charismatic theory of catholicity maintains that the Church exists wherever the Holy Spirit acts, and that the presence and action of the Holy Spirit can be subjectively established by those who pretend to be inspired and guided by the Holy Spirit. From the Orthodox point of view, the manifestations of the Holy Spirit are never separated from the Holy Trinity, from Jesus Christ and from the Church, which was founded by Christ and by the Holy Spirit Himself. Nor can they be separated from divine revelation in the Holy Scriptures and in Holy Tradition. According to the ancient precepts of tradition, all those who refer to the Holy Spirit must prove that their life and doctrine are in agreement with the spirit of the Church, and that whatever they ascribe to the Holy Spirit conforms with the revelation of Jesus Christ and the Holy Spirit, in the authenticity of which the Orthodox Church has no doubts.

The understanding of catholicity in the so-called "branch" theory is unacceptable for Orthodoxy because of the very understanding of what these branches are. What this theory recognizes as being branches of the Church are from our point of view broken and separated from the tree. The Church cannot be comprised of branches that are separated from her. These broken branches keep certain characteristics of the tree, but their existence is deformed by the inoculation of other principles alien to the Church. A pile of broken branches cannot produce catholicity.

The evolutionary theory of catholicity has the same defect. The growth of the Church in time does not break her body in pieces. The body of the Church develops, but does not change in nature. Such was a very pertinent teaching of St. Vincent of Lérins. If a new generation of Christians rebuilds Christianity in its own way, it separates itself from the Church and is no longer included in her catholicity. To conform to or to adopt the conditions, spirit and culture of the given time is no justification. The Church can adjust her methods of spreading Christianity to the special conditions of the time, but nothing else must be changed for the sake of such an adjustment. In everything that has at least some importance in Christianity, it is not the Church that must adapt herself to man or to the times, but it is man, with the help of the Church, who must strive to assimilate and realize the eternal Christianity of Christ both in his personal and common life.

The catholicity in minimalism, which is very popular in the ecumenical movement, contradicts the very nature of Christianity, which is essentially maximalistic. Jesus Christ calls us to the perfection of the heavenly Father for the transfiguration of the whole universe in God. The advent of Christ and the descent of the Holy Spirit were accomplished in order to grant to us the fulness of existence, which mankind had never possessed, even in the Old Testament Church. To narrow Christianity to any minimum means therefore to betray its basic ideal.

The newest theory of catholicity in the ecumenical movement sees the principle of the unity of the Church in her relationship with the world. But in this fallen world, unity either does not exist or consists of evil, or in the best case it has a clearly worldly character and thus is foreign to the Church. Christ came to unite the world; now we are called upon to unite the body of Christ with the powers of the fallen world. If the unifying power of the Church is considered to be in her mission in the world, we must state that this mission itself must be derived from the unity of the Church. Its mission in the world can be a constitutive principle of Christianity or of the Church. In addition, it is important to remember that the very purpose of the Christian mission in the world is to bring all men out from this world into the Kingdom of Christ.

Some Theological Reflections on Chalcedon

There may be various approaches to the Chalcedonian oros. First, it has a great religious significance, but it also is of great value for scientific theology. Truth, revealed in dogmas, determines the whole life of the Church. Theology is called to give the most accurate, rational definition of truth, to lay it out systematically and explain its contents. In this manner, theology satisfies the just desire of Christians for knowledge and forges weapons against heresies, which can only be surmounted by a precise and deepened knowledge of truth.

The most essential part of the Chalcedonian definition is expressed by the council in the following words:

> Therefore, following the holy fathers, we all with one accord teach men to acknowledge one and the same Son, our Lord Jesus Christ, at once complete in Godhead and complete in manhood, truly God and truly man, consisting also of a reasonable soul and body; of one substance [*homoousios*] with the Father as regards His Godhead, and at the same time of one substance with us as regards His manhood; like us in all respects, apart from sin; as regards his Godhead, begotten of the Father before the ages, but yet as regards His manhood begotten, for us men and for our salvation, of the Virgin Mary, the Theotokos; one and the same Christ, Son, Lord, Only-begotten, recognized in two natures, without confusion, without change, without division, without separation.

The Chalcedonian dogma solemnly confirms that Christ is the Son of God, true God Who truly became man. One and the same Christ, our Lord and Savior, is indeed God and man. The religious significance of this doctrine is immense, inasmuch as all our faith in salvation rests on the conviction that Christ is both God and man: salvation is impossible if Christ is only God or only man.[1]

Let us imagine that Christ was only man. Can a man, even if he is without sin, save all mankind—i.e., assume in his being all men; surmount and ransom all their faults and sins; transform them in himself; become an ideal image of man, perfect love, truth and holiness; unite all with God and with each other? Obviously, this is beyond the capabilities of any man, especially one weakened by sin, as all men are. Only God, born as man among fallen mankind, could communicate to His human nature the all-embracing power of salvation.

On the other hand, if salvation is essentially a complete cleansing and transfiguration of man and the transformation of fallen mankind into a new creation, then it could only be possible through man himself, from within his nature. Someone, originating from old Adam, must have become a new Adam, the source of the renewed mankind. Thus, the Savior, being God, must also have been a man.

However, the union in Christ of the divine and the human, which is evident from the New Testament and substantiated by the Council of Chalcedon, could not but call forth many questions. In the first place, is such a miraculous union possible? Does it not appear imaginary? Should it not be substantially limited in its meaning? In the second place, if it is true, then how is it possible? How can it be explained, and on what basis can it be established? The possibility of the union of God and man in Christ was rejected or limited by a whole series of heresies, just as it is denied today by unbelievers and "semibelievers." Patristic theology successfully defended the faith in the God-manhood of Christ. First of all, the Church could not but see a historical event in the incarnation. The witness of Christ Himself and of the apostolic Church, preserved in scripture and tradition, could be reinterpreted (and

[1]See, for example, St. Leo the Great's *Tome to Flavian* 5.

misunderstood), but its meaning is clear for the unbiased mind: "the Word became flesh" (John 1:14); the Son of God was born of a woman (Galatians 4:4), from "the seed of David" (Romans 1:3) and became Emmanuel (Matthew 1:23). Our Lord obtained the Church with His own blood (Acts 20:28)—the "Author of life" (Acts 3:15), "the Lord of glory" was crucified (1 Corinthians 2:8). He Who descended from heaven was the Son of Man (John 3:13). Or, in the words of Ignatius of Antioch, the "God-bearer," the pupil of the apostles: "Our Lord Jesus Christ is God in flesh, true Life in death, from Mary and from God, the Son of Man and the Son of God."[2]

It is indeed noteworthy that the early Church experienced the fact of our salvation with such strength that this very fact served as an obvious proof of the truth of the incarnation. For if the salvation of men has been and is being fulfilled and yet is impossible without our Savior having been truly God and truly man, then Christ is God-man. This is the foundation of the well-known "soteriological argument," which the fathers directed against the gnostics, the Arians, the Apollinarians, the Nestorians and other heretics. The incarnation does not contradict the divine dignity and does not violate the distinction between the divine and the human. Having created the world, God, in His creative and providential power and wisdom, is present in the world and in each creature. The divine Logos, through Whom God the Father created everything, and Who is inseparable from the creation, did not pollute Himself by personally assuming that sinless nature which He Himself created.[3] If God is love, then it is natural for the Son of God to have come on earth to save lost and perishing man. The incarnation is not disgraceful for God, and even the death on the cross glorifies the unlimited and lifegiving love of God, for the sake of which Christ offers the sacrifice of redemption (cf John 13:31-32; 1 John 4:9; Romans 5:8). Creation is not a stranger to God: it is conformed to God, and from the beginning, in paradise, man was called to perfect communion with God. In Christ, in the

[2]*To Polycarp* 3.
[3]See St. Athanasius, *On the Incarnation* 41, 42.

hypostatic union of God with man, this communion is fulfilled.

At the same time, the divine and human natures in Christ do not mix, and one does not become the other. Moreover, the interpenetration and "adhesion" of the divine and human in Christ has its limits, inasmuch as even the most perfect human nature, being created, is essentially limited and cannot be equal to the divine nature. Thus, the idea of the incarnation does not lead us to that absurd and religiously intolerable conclusion that the absolute, divine Spirit is identified or is somehow equated with the limited, created nature of man.

To the question of how it is possible for Christ to be born God and man, Orthodox theology answers first that it is possible for God to be in the most intimate relation with the creation, and secondly and mainly with the doctrine of the unity of person in Christ notwithstanding His two natures.

The first point was partially discussed above. God is, in fact, united with creation, and in Christ His oneness with it reaches its fulness. There is nothing unbecoming or contradictory to God in this union. It must be added that Holy Scripture and Orthodox Tradition have always maintained this point of view. God is not a prisoner of His own transcendent perfection and absoluteness. He can, while remaining absolute in Himself, condescend to creation in His creative ideas and energies, in His Word, theophanies, revelations and grace.[4] The incarnation is the most perfect condescension of God to creation: the Wisdom of God, in the words of St. Paul, became "our wisdom" (1 Corinthians 1:30). "For in Him dwelleth all the fulness of the Godhead bodily" (Colossians 2:9). The Word of God was revealed in the word of man; He Who was the image of God was revealed in the image of man.

But let us rather consider the doctrine of the oneness of Christ's hypostasis.[5] There is in Christ one hypostasis or person and two natures or essences. We must consequently distinguish person from essence and allow the possibility of a union of

---

[4]The whole Orthodox teaching concerning the divine Logos and the Holy Spirit confirms this. This doctrine was particularly developed by St. Gregory Palamas.

[5]In Christian theology, "hypostasis" can be terminologically equated with "person," and "nature" with "essence."

two different natures in one person. Space does not allow us to dwell too long on the concept of essence in patristics. Under the influence of Greek philosophy, we find two meanings of "substance" in the fathers. One reflects the Aristotelian *prima substantia,* meaning a being taken in its complete, independent existence. The second implies the essential content and the totality of the necessary properties of any given being. Thus, one can call every man a being because he possesses the human nature or essence common to all men. It would be more accurate to call "being" the whole mankind, in its polypersonal unity.[6] Indeed, in connection with the trinitarian discussions of the fourth century there arose in patristic thought the idea of one, yet polyhypostatic, consubstantial being. Thus, God is one trihypostatic being, having one essence. The fathers applied the idea of consubstantiality also to mankind. The Chalcedonian oros mentions Christ as consubstantial with mankind.

Let us now consider the concept of person. Greek philosophy was interested in the general rather than the particular or the individual.[7] For it, the general in being rather than the individual seemed the more perfect, valuable and permanent. Typical in this respect is Anaximander, for whom the desire for a personal existence is a sort of sin. Greek philosophy knew, of course, the fact of individual existence, but it either explained it by the stability of concrete substances capable of activity, or formally defined the individual as a subject with a particular characteristic (Stoics). It is noteworthy that the *principium individuationis* for Greek philosophy lies traditionally in matter—i.e., from the point of view of the Greek philosophers themselves, in the lowest if not negative entity.

The fathers of the Church obviously could not depend on Greek philosophy in their teaching about the person. Terminologically, the word *persona* first appeared in the sense of person in the West (from the third century) and then in the East (from the fourth century, as *prosopon*). The word

[6] This disturbs western theologians, who are much more "individualistic" than eastern ones.

[7] The general, as the principle of active life, was called "nature" by the Greek philosophers.

"hypostasis" at first had a broad meaning of a concrete reality. From the middle of the fourth century it began to be used in the sense of "person," primarily in triadology. After Chalcedon it began to be used in the same sense in Christology and in theology in general.

In patristics, the most popular doctrines about the person are those of Leontius of Byzantium and John of Damascus. The first had a valuable doctrine of *enhypostasis* (of which more is stated below), but the whole perspective of Leontius is borrowed, to his own misfortune, from Greek philosophy.[8] More or less the same can be said about John of Damascus. Many excellent ideas can be found in his writings, but he does not have a complete, systematic teaching on the "person."[9] Other fathers have their own definitions and characterizations.

One can briefly summarize the patristic doctrine on the person by stating that the person or hypostasis is the particular mode of existence of each being.[10] It is in no case a part of being, which would be separated from everything else in the being.[11] It is a particular principle of existence which embraces the whole being and pervades everything with itself, making everything personal or actual, or, in other words, belonging to this person. In this respect, the hypostasis is the principle corresponding to the essence, which also is not part of being but the mode of its existence.[12] The hypostasis is the principle of existence and life.[13] This means that the nonhypostatical

[8]See especially his *Against Nestorius and Eutyches.*
[9]See his *Philosophical Chapters* and *On the Orthodox Faith.*
[10]See St. Basil the Great, *On the Holy Spirit* 16; Didymus, *On the Trinity* 1:9, 2:1; St. John of Damascus, *On the Orthodox Faith* 1:8, 3:5 (PG 95: 136); Theodore Abu-Qurra, *Opuscula,* disp. 28. On the place of Amphilochius of Iconium, see K. Holl, *Amphilochius von Ikonium* (Tübingen, 1904); and Sallet, "La Theologie d'Amphiloque," *Bulletin de Littérature Ecclésiastique* (1905).
[11]See John of Damascus, *On the Orthodox Faith* 3:6.
[12]See Basil the Great, *Letter* 38 2:4.
[13]For example, see Athanasius, *Tome to the Antiochenes* (PG 26:796); *Against the Arians* 4:1; St. Gregory of Nyssa, *On Common Notions* (PG 45:184); St. Cyril of Alexandria, *On the Gospel of John* 5:5; Leontius of Byzantium, *Against Nestorius and Eutyches* (PG 86:1280); St. Maximus the Confessor, *Theological and Polemical Writings* (PG 91:261, 264); Anastasius Sinaita, *The Guide* 9; John of Damascus, *On Two Wills* 4; *Dialectic* 10, 11, 17, 18, 29, 44, 45, 65, 66; *On the Orthodox Faith* 3:9.

cannot exist; it can be thought of only as an abstract possibility. In reality, the nonpersonal does not exist: everything
belongs to some person. The hypostasis is the carrier of existence, the subject of life—the one who lives.[14]

This does not mean that existence or life comes from the
person or is created by it *ex nihilo,* but according to the deepest thought of Christian theology, each being, each individual,
must have as the focal point, the carrier of its own existence,
the one who possesses and controls its own being. The person
is precisely the principle and the center of everything in the
being. By its very morphosis the word "hypostasis" implies
that which underlies a thing, that by which anything subsists
or exists.[15] It is like a base of support of the whole being and
all its contents. A hypostasis can proceed from another hypostasis (and only from it, and not from something impersonal),
but once it has come into being it is a "self-existing," "self-
supporting" being.[16] Thus, Christ says that He has "life in
Himself," even if He has it from the Father (John 5:26).
The hypostasis, in its logical aspect, is also the subject of
whatever can be said about any given being.[17] John of Damascus writes that strictly speaking there exists only the hypostasis.
As to essence, it has its being in the hypostasis, so the real
subject of existence is the hypostasis.[18] Hence the conviction
of the fathers that if an essence has no hypostasis of its own
it has to be "enhypostasized," i.e., it belongs to some other
hypostasis. Thus, the human body is hypostasized by the
spiritual person of man, and the human nature in Christ is
hypostasized by the person of the Son of God.[19]

The essence is possessed by the hypostasis. The latter is
the carrier of all attributes and the principle of the whole

[14]See John of Damascus, *Dialectic* 5.
[15]John of Damascus, *Dialectic* 43.
[16]Basil the Great, *Letter* 236 6; St. Gregory of Nazianzus, *Oration* 33 16;
John of Damascus, *Dialectic* 5, 30, 39, 43, 44, 46; *On the Orthodox Faith*
1:6, 7, 3:6; Theorianos, *Disputation with the Armenian Catholicos* (PG
133:125). Cf the *Dictionnaire de théologie catholique* 7:404.
[17]See Gregory of Nyssa, *Against Eunomius* (PG 45:308).
[18]*On the Orthodox Faith* 1:8, 3:6; *Dialectic* 42.
[19]See Leontius of Byzantium (in PG 86:1277); Maximus the Confessor,
Theological and Polemical Writings (PG 91:150); John of Damascus, *Dialectic*
44; *On the Orthodox Faith* 3:9.

activity of the being.[20] It is the principle of freedom, movement, action.[21] It is the principle of intelligence and thought.[22]
In the person, the principle of life, the active and passive
aspects, must be distinguished. The person actualizes and
determines the concrete content of life and also the given
state of the being. To live and to be active in this way or
in another way, to be in that or in another condition, depends
—according to the possibilities given by nature—only on the
person. At the same time, the person is the focal point of all
the experiences of any given being: only the person experiences, apprehends, accepts, perceives and feels.

If the hypostasis is the foundation of existence and life,
the carrier of all attributes of the being and of its very essence,
then it is understandable that Orthodox theology, both in
triadology and Christology, as even Roman Catholic scholars
like to point out,[23] always stresses primarily the persons of
God the Father, Son and Holy Spirit, in which it apprehends,
in a living and concrete way, all Their divine perfections and
in Christ His human attributes.

The hypostasis is the principle of inner unity of each
being; it is the principle of identity. Long before Chalcedon,
the fathers constantly underlined that being God and man,
Christ is "one and the same." Chalcedon defined that that
which makes Christ one and the same in two natures is His
hypostasis. The hypostasis is indivisible in itself, a concrete
indivisibility.[24] It conveys unity to everything in the being it
hypostasizes, for everything in its being belongs to it. The
essence is one because it is hypostatic. In general, the hypostasis
is the principle of wholeness, the whole in itself. In it are

[20]John of Damascus, *Dialectic* 42, 44, 66; *On the Orthodox Faith* 3:6;
Suidas, "Hypostasis," in *Lexicon*.

[21]Gregory of Nyssa, *Catechesis* 1; John of Damascus, *On the Orthodox
Faith* 1:7, 8. See the latter's definition of God: "Persona est naturae ration-
alis individua substantia."

[22]Gregory of Nazianzus, *Oration 33* 16; Gregory of Nyssa, *On Common
Notions* (PG 45:184).

[23]This is, for example, a central idea in Th. de Régnon's excellent book
Etudes de thèologie positive sur la Sainte Trinité.

[24]This justifies the "rapprochement" between person and *individuum*, for
the latter, as "indivisible," acquires its indestructible wholeness from its person—the unique center of its existence.

united, as in a focal center, all the attributes and actions of the being.[25] Therefore, the person is the principle of the so-called *communicatio idiomatum,* i.e., the possibility for two natures included in one hypostasis to mutually share their properties.[26] Thus, in man, the body can become spiritualized, and the soul can suffer the tribulations of the body as its own. Thus, in Christ, man assumes the powers and perfections of God, and God lives in conformity with the man. The "communion of natures" is possible without their hypostatical unity, but in such unity it becomes full, natural and necessary.

If the hypostasis is the focal point of all the forms of experience of the being, it cannot but acquire a certain plurality. This led the fathers to the idea of the composite hypostasis.[27] In the heretical interpretation of this idea, the hypostasis was nothing else but a sum of two natures, a sum of their addition. But since the existence of an ahypostatical nature is ontologically impossible, Nestorius came to the conclusion that Christ possesses a composite hypostasis, or "πρόσωπον τῆς ἑνώσεως," which is the sum of the hypostases of the divine and human natures of Christ in some common subject composed of His divine and human attributes. The "πρόσωπον τῆς ἑνώσεως" is only an addition of heteronomous elements, not the one self-identical center of Christ's being.[28] This doctrine was condemned by the Church. A mere union of two persons cannot result in one person, but only in a relationship of both. Besides, the identity of two persons is as ontologically impossible as an impersonal essence. Theodore of Mopsuestia was more logical than Nestorius when he suggested the analogy of a marriage to the union of

[25]See Dionysius of Alexandria (in Mansi 1:1044); Athanasius, *Against Apollinaris* 1:12; Epiphanius of Cyprus, *Heresies* 77:29; *Ancoratus;* Rusticus, *Disputations against the Acephaloi* (PL 47:1239); John of Damascus, *Dialectic* 37, 42, 65, 66; Suidas, *Lexicon.*

[26]See, for example, Athanasius, *Letter to Adelphius* 3; Gregory of Nyssa, *Against Eunomius* (PG 45:705, 697); Gregory of Nazianzus, *Oration* 38 13; Cyril of Alexandria, *Anathema* 4; Leo the Great, *Tome to Flavian* 5; John of Damascus, *On the Orthodox Faith* 3:4, 7.

[27]See John of Damascus, *Dialectic* 10, 41, 44, 48, 65, 66; *On the Orthodox Faith* 3:3-7, 4:5; Leo the Great, *Tome to Flavian* 3.

[28]See Nestorius, *Book of Heraclides,* and the studies by Jugie and Loofs.

God and man in Christ.[29] But such a union cannot be called a hypostatic union, for the husband and wife are not one person.

Consequently, the composite hypostasis of which the fathers speak can only be understood as a participation of one person in the existence of other natures hypostasized by it. Hypostasis is not nearly so much complex in itself as its existence may be complex and pluralistic. Thus, Christ's hypostasis lives both a divine and a human life in all their complexity, thus becoming complex itself.

Two persons cannot be identified as one,[30] because the person is particular, exclusive, unrepeatable, unique and indivisible.[31] As a self-identity, the person cannot become another person or two persons, just as a mathematical point cannot be divided in two. However, in a person as such there is no limitation: it is neither a thing, nor a substance, nor a part of a substance, nor a faculty. It is simply the first principle and the foundation of existence, and as such is open to all that exists.[32] Therefore, each person can partake of the life of all; it can be in other hypostases (just as the Son of God abides in the Father and the Father in the Son); it can live the life of another (as Christ lived and continues to live in our life). But the person always remains itself and does not mix with others. Hypostasis is "self" (*auto*), self-existing, self-being, etc.[33] The same thought was expressed by the fathers, who said that persons were numerically distinct: they can be counted as units.[34] St. Basil the Great, however, very wisely pointed out that it is better not to count but to name

[29]*On the Incarnation,* fragment 8 (PG 46:981).

[30]John of Damascus, *Dialectic* 66.

[31]Basil the Great, *Letter 38* (PG 32:328); *Letter 236* 6; *Against Eunomius* 1:10, 2:28, 4; Gregory of Nazianzus, *Oration 33* 16; Leontius of Byzantium, *A Resolution of the Arguments Advanced by Severus* (PG 86:1915); *Against Nestorius and Eutyches* (PG 86:1280); John of Damascus, *On Two Wills* 4; *Dialectic* 10, 11, 29, 42, 45, 65; *On the Orthodox Faith* 1:8, 12, 14; 3:5.

[32]John of Damascus, *On the Orthodox Faith* 1:7, 8; 3:8.

[33]See Dionysius of Alexandria (in Mansi 1:1044); Gregory of Nazianzus, *Oration 33* 16; John of Damascus, *Dialectic* 42.

[34]Gregory of Nazianzus, *Oration 33* 16; Leontius of Byzantium, *Against Nestorius and Eutyches* (PG 86:1281); John of Damascus, *Dialectic* 5, 10, 16, 43; *On the Orthodox Faith* 3:6.

hypostases, for units are impersonal but in names the unique distinction of each person is expressed. As the principle of an independent existence, the person is the bearer of independence and freedom: if it does not create its own life, it can, in any case, determine it. As the particular and the exclusive, the hypostasis is radically distinct from the essence, which is primarily the common and the objective. If the hypostasis can unite everything in itself, it does so only "for itself," subjectively. Objectively or ontologically, it unites with others through its nature.

Each hypostasis is determined by its special, personal characteristics.[35] Triadology reveals that the personal character of a hypostasis is determined by its relation to other hypostases, by its special place or function in the common existence. And this is rooted in the procession of one hypostasis from another. Obviously, in personal relations the individual characteristic of each person is expressed. All other personal characteristics are either external or more or less accidental or common to many persons. Yet it is supremely important to distinguish the hypostasis as such from its attributes, even from its personal characteristics. The hypostasis possesses attributes and is determined by them in life. It finds its expression in them, but it is not identified with them, for it is their carrier and the principle of their existence.[36] Identification of the person with its attributes results either in the reduction of the person to a particular act of its life (e.g., conscience, free will) or to individual character, or to the identification of the person with its relation to another person. Thus, for example, scholastic theology identifies the hypostasis of God the Father with fatherhood, the hypostasis of the Son of God with sonship, etc. Obviously, the relationship cannot be the principle or the origin of existence. It itself implies a foundation of the one who is in relation with the other. Relationship is activity or state, but not the hypostasis. The opinion of many philosophers and psychologists that the person is consciousness

[35]Basil the Great, *Letter 34* 3-4; Leontius of Byzantium, *A Resolution of the Arguments Advanced by Severus* (PG 86:1917); John of Damascus, *Dialectic* 13, 29, 30; *On the Orthodox Faith* 1:8, 3:6.
[36]See Petravius, *On the Trinity* 4:8, 5-10.

or freedom or a special individual character is superficial, false
and incompatible with the patristic idea that will and reason
are related to the nature and not to the person, and that the
person is not an expression but the foundation of individual
existence.

Logically, it is better to define each given person by its
particular function in relation to others, by names or personal
pronouns (I, you, he, who, but not "it" or "some" or "something"[37]). Every attempt to define person by the general
concept results in a misunderstanding, because general concepts imply essences and not persons. The very general concept
of person is an abstraction, a generalization of our reason. In
fact, there exists only the plurality of unique persons and not
a "person-in-general." Augustine was embarrassed by the very
existence of such a generic concept,[38] for an abstraction is not
a reality.

The influence of Greek philosophy on the fathers was so
great that they sometimes defined hypostasis as if it were an
individual. St. Basil the Great and Leontius of Byzantium
sometimes wrote that hypostasis is the essence plus personal
attributes. John of Damascus wrote that hypostasis is a "lower
form" or "circumscription" of nature, i.e., a limited essence.[39]
The identification of person with *individuum* is impossible, for
then God would become three individuals, and would be
three Gods and not one God. Christ, then, would be separated
from both the Trinity and mankind. Being a person, Christ has
no particular essence as distinct from the Trinity, and the
limitation of the human nature of Christ from the nature of
other men is but relative: Christ is not only *homoiousion* but
homoousion to the whole of mankind. Properly understood,
patristic tradition maintains that hypostasis is neither essence
nor the *individuum,* but is the principle and the foundation
of the individual existence of essence. Person is to nature what

[37]See Gregory of Nazianzus (in PG 37:180); John of Damascus, *Dialectic*
8; *On the Orthodox Faith* 3:7.

[38]*On the Trinity* 3:7:48-9.

[39]Basil the Great, *Letter 236* 6; *Against Eunomius* 1:10, 2:27, 4:1; Leontius of Byzantium (in PG 86:1915, 1280, 1281, 1301); Maximus the Confessor, *Theological and Polemical Writings* (PG 91:153, 260); John of
Damascus, *On Two Wills* 4; *Dialectic* 10, 11, 29, 44, 65.

the principle of being and life is to their content; what the foundation of all attributes and actions is to the latter; what the particular and unique is to the common; what the subjective is to the objective. The person possesses the essence; the essence abides in the hypostasis.[40] The real content of the hypostasis is in its essence, and therefore, without essence it is void and nonexistent. As to the essence, it has no foundation and no life. Without the person it becomes a mere potentiality.

We know that one person can hypostasize, i.e., contain in itself and give life to, two natures, which then become indivisibly united in one being. The Son of God after the incarnation never ceases to be man. The person is capable of hypostasizing another nature, because the person is open and not limited, and this is precisely its distinctive feature. It can assume in its life that which does not belong to its own nature. However, it is to be noted that the person always has a special tie with one of the natures which it hypostasizes, namely with the highest of the two (in Christ with divinity, in man with the soul). The person does not stand between two natures, but being rooted in the higher of the two, it elevates the lower nature to the higher, and carries the higher nature into the lower. The person, as the foundation of existence, is the deepest element in the being, and it is naturally connected with what is the deepest part of each being, which is its spirituality.

In contrast with Greek philosophy, Orthodox theology considers the person as the highest value and the principle of perfection.[41] The more perfect is the being, the more perfect is the person. There is a hypostatical principle in everything that exists, even in material things,[42] but its paramount expression is in the spiritual.

[40]See Basil the Great, *Letter 236* 6; *Against Eunomius* 1:10, 2:27, 4:1; Gregory of Nyssa, *Against Eunomius* 1; *On Common Notions* (PG 45:182); *Catechesis* 1; Augustine, *On the Trinity* 8:6:11; Maximus the Confessor (in PG 91:153, 260); John of Damascus, *On the Orthodox Faith* 3:3, 4, 6, 9; *Dialectic* 30; Theodore Abu-Qurra, *Opuscula*, disp. 11; Suidas, "Hypostasis," in *Lexicon;* Theorianos, *Disputation with the Armenian Catholicos* (PG 133: 132-133).
[41]See Gregory of Nazianzus, *Oration 33* 16.
[42]John of Damascus affirms this on several occasions in his *Philosophical Chapters.*